God in the Garden

Discovering the Spiritual Riches of Gardening

A WEEK-BY-WEEK JOURNEY
THROUGH THE
CHRISTIAN YEAR

Maureen Gilmer

LOYOLAPRESS.

CHICAGO

LOYOLAPRESS.

3441 N. ASHLAND AVENUE
CHICAGO, ILLINOIS 60657

Cover photos courtesy of Maureen Gilmer
Interior design by Nick Panos
Author photo by Stanley Kramer

Library of Congress Cataloging-in-Publication Data

Gilmer, Maureen.
God in the garden : discovering the spiritual riches of gardening : a week-by-week journey through the Christian year /Maureen Gilmer.
p. cm.
Includes bibliographical references.
ISBN 0-8294-1688-9
1. Gardeners—Religious life. 2. Gardens—Religious aspects—Christianity—Meditations. 3. Spiritual life—Catholic Church—Meditations. I. Title.
BV4596.G36 G55 2002
242'.2—dc21

2002003573

Printed in Canada
02 03 04 05 06 Webcom 10 9 8 7 6 5 4 3 2 1

Dedication

With fond affection this book is dedicated to Rev. Leon Juchniewicz.
Ut eis in ministerio mansuetudinem, in actione sollertiam et in oratione constantiam concedere digneris.

Contents

Acknowledgments

My sincerest gratitude to my agent, Jeanne Fredericks, and all her careful work with Loyola editor Vinita Wright, who first saw the potential in this book. Many heartfelt thanks to managing editor Rebecca Johnson and all the others at Loyola Press whose work has made my prose read far better than it was written. Creating a book is such a team effort, and the author is only one small part of this equation.

Introduction

I BELIEVE GOD TOLD US IN THE BEGINNING exactly where we would find happiness with him on Earth. When God created humans in his own image, he did not choose to place them on a mountaintop, in the ocean, in a building or cave. No, God chose a garden as the ideal place, a paradise in which his beloved creations Adam and Eve should live. He even gave it a name, Eden, and it was filled with plants of every kind, fruits and vegetables, and rivers of sweet, flowing water.

Then God told Adam and Eve what they were to do in that garden. He directly charged them with the task of cultivating and tending the plants of Eden. In paradise, where we might imagine indolent leisure as the ideal way to live, God puts Adam and Eve to work.

My happiest, most satisfied moments are those spent working in the garden. There is something primal that makes digging and planting and watering a nearly spiritual act. In the quiet of labor, my mind is free to contemplate life—with its beauty, frustration, and sadness. In those hours I feel closest to God and my mind opens to receive him.

I am not alone. Gardeners, farmers, and naturalists since ancient times have experienced the same indefinable closeness to a higher power when faced with the simple synergy of earth and plants. I have come to believe there is something more profound at work that makes us yearn to garden. Perhaps it is because plant life is created by God and thus imbued with his presence. When we work with plants, we become closer to this presence, working hand in hand with God.

This yearning to be with God in the garden is rooted in Scripture and in the parables of Jesus that are based on pastoral, agrarian life in the Holy Land. It was clearly understood by St. Phocas in the third century, St. Francis in the fourteenth, and St. Thérèse in the nineteenth. It is revealed to us through Marian apparitions and Christian garden shrines around the world. Even modern science finds its place in this path of the spirit, for as Mendel the monk discovered the secrets of genetics, and the missionary botanists brought new and wonderful plants into our world, we too may reconcile science and creation in the garden.

Since my introduction to horticulture nearly twenty-five years ago, I have found myriad connections between plants and religion. I began to recognize a new dimension of gardening that is more than mere technique or science. Early Christianity was rich in botanical symbols that were readily understood by the farmers who made up much of society at the time. The pastoral Hebrew traditions of the Old Testament and the parables of Jesus in the New use plants, both wild and cultivated, as a means of communicating spiritual truths. In the first centuries, the Roman church inherited the former empire's rich agricultural knowledge and texts. In the Middle Ages, this knowledge was largely preserved by cloistered monastic communities, which cultivated vital plants while fallow fields outside followed Europe into chaos.

The modern Catholic faith has an immense wealth of earthy spiritual traditions. The liturgy and calendar of feast days have clear parallels to the farmer's annual cycle of reaping and sowing. The sacraments themselves are rooted in wheat grass, grapevines, olive trees, and aromatic resins. Sacramentals such as the rosary are connected to Mary through scented flowers. Many of our most beloved saints are linked to specific plants, such as the shamrock of St. Patrick and St. Johnswort of John the Baptist.

Many of these plant connections were gradually dropped from Christianity as ours became a less agrarian and more industrialized society. Most Catholics don't realize that the seasons of the liturgy are a reflection of those in the fields. As Christians we are fortunate, for we have two thousand years of agricultural symbolism and celebration to unearth in our vast history of forgotten devotions.

The pages of this book lay out the seasonal connections of faith to nature, with the week-by-week structure linking what is heard in church to what one does in the garden. The gardening activities are then tied to Scripture and to brief meditations by gardeners throughout history. Monthly and weekly features on plants reveal the Christian significance of that particular plant so that we begin to see more than just green leaves in a landscape.

My hope for this book is that it will help readers rediscover a path of Christianity that is age-old. As our days become more harried and filled with technostuff that promises to simplify our life, it is essential that we seek true wisdom and simplicity through a deeper relationship with God in the garden. Above all, I hope that this book helps everyone find tranquility as I have, born of muddy knees and green-stained fingers.

Wander out into the garden of our Lord. Leave behind your struggles with technology, money, family, and traffic. Enter a space that is quiet, peaceful, and most of all, alive. Treasure the plants as God's most peaceful, beautiful creations. Discover the miraculous interconnectedness of all living things. Celebrate diversity and embark on a lifelong learning experience. Come dwell in your own private Eden, and in tending it, fulfill the destiny set down for you in the first verses of Genesis.

January

Lily of the Valley
Convallaria majalis
Zone 3
Type: Hardy bulb
Origin: Europe
Habitat: Shade or part shade
Size: About 12 inches tall and as wide
Plant: Fall, from dormant bulbs
Notable feature: Fragrant, bell-shaped white flowers

Lily of the Valley

Convallaria majalis

Lily of the valley is among the spring-blooming flowers. Its white flowers came to represent the purity of the Virgin Mary, and its sweet scent her love. This plant also came to symbolize the immaculate conception. This old-fashioned flower came into cultivation in sixteenth-century Europe, and it is native throughout that continent and Asia Minor. It is valued among the few bulbs that flourish in the shade, and it easily naturalizes in forested garden settings.

The woman answered the serpent: "We may eat of the fruit of the trees in the garden; it is only about the fruit of the tree in the middle of the garden that God said, 'You shall not eat it or even touch it, lest you die.'" But the serpent said to the woman: "You certainly will not die! No, God knows well that the moment you eat of it your eyes will be opened and you will be like gods who know what is good and what is bad." The woman saw that the tree was good for food, pleasing to the eyes, and desirable for gaining wisdom. So she took some of its fruit and ate it; and she also gave some to her husband, who was with her, and he ate it. Then the eyes of both of them were opened, and they realized that they were naked; so they sewed fig leaves together and made loincloths for themselves.

GENESIS 3:2–7

January

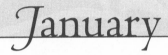

first week

Meditation

As fallible human beings, we make mistakes that we hope will not be as grievous as that of Adam and Eve. But failures in the garden should not be considered a sin. Rather, think of them as opportunities for you to improve your garden. Early January is a good time to sit quietly and think about your plants and garden, discerning exactly what went wrong. Even if you plan on doing little more than laying out a row of tomato plants, you should strive to lay it out better than last season's row of tomatoes.

One of the great truths of gardening, and of life for that matter, is that we learn far more from what we do wrong than from what we do right! If you are told not to water the leaves of the plants in the sun, this advice might go in one ear and out the other. But if you do so and permanently spoil the green foliage of your squash or rhododendrons, you aren't likely to make that mistake again. Therefore, spend these winter days assessing your garden's strengths and weaknesses; then do some reading or talk with other gardeners, and begin to formulate a plan for the upcoming season.

*The most noteworthy thing about gardeners is that they are always optimistic, always
enterprising, and never satisfied. They are forever planting, and forever digging up.
They always look forward to doing better than they have ever done before.
"Next year . . ." they say, and even as they pronounce the words you become infected
by their enthusiasm and allow yourself to be persuaded that the garden will indeed
look different, quite different, next year. Experience tells you that it never does, but
how poor and disheartening a thing is experience compared with hope!*

Vita Sackville-West, *Country Notes,* **1939**

Gardening

A garden is an environment where plants gather together to create a sense
of place. More important, that place is where human beings may dwell to
their benefit and enjoyment. To retreat into one's garden after a hectic day
at the office is to engage in an act of healing in which we tend the damage
inflicted by a brutal world.

Garden design is all about creating places for retreat, and the design itself
is alive, changing with time as plants mature to influence that space in different ways. This is a good month to conjure up new design ideas for the
garden. Go back through last year's gardening magazines and study the pictures at length. Is there anything you see that might be adapted to your home
landscape? Is there an easier way to build it? Are there plants featured that
you would like to grow? Even though you may lack design training, you can
add new plants or replace old ones with those that will be more satisfying.

It is always best to start redesigning your garden by focusing on what
problems need to be solved and how they might be resolved in an aestheti-
cally pleasing manner. Does an eyesore need to be covered up? Try vines, or
plant a bamboo or yew screen. Would you like to add color to a dark, shady
corner? Explore the effects of brightly variegated foliage plants that give the
illusion of dappled sunlight. Does your garden lack a focal point, leaving you
bewildered as to what to look at much of the time? Choose a special tree, a
work of art, a fountain, or a birdbath to become the center of your planting scheme. Before you plant anything this coming year, strive to solve these
problems first.

Pussy Willow

Salix discolor

You'll find this species of willow growing wild all over the eastern United States, concentrated along the waterways, where they are valuable erosion control plants. We might not give this plant a second look if it weren't for the soft, silver-gray buds that swell in the spring. They are actually catkins, a wind-pollinated reproductive structure that contains male and female parts.

For centuries people have cut switches of pussy willow and brought them indoors during this time of the year. If placed in water in the warmth of your home, the buds will swell into the beautiful textured rods sold by all the swanky florists. Pussy willow is easy to grow in the home garden, so you can cut your own rods each year without going into the countryside. Use them along fence lines or as background foliage plants that won't be front and center if you cut them to use indoors. Plants will require plenty of moisture to produce the long, slender whips that make the best cutting material. Buy pussy willows bare root in fall or spring, or purchase them as container-grown stock. Since willows root so easily, a six-inch-long dormant cutting taken in spring and placed in damp sand will easily root in just a few weeks.

Pussy Willow

Salix discolor

Zone 3

Type: Deciduous shrub or small tree

Origin: Wetlands of eastern North America

Habitat: Moist soil in sun or part shade

Size: To 10 feet tall and 6 to 10 feet wide

Plant: Fall or spring, bare root or from containers

Notable feature: Fuzzy spring buds

God grant me the serenity to accept the things I cannot change, the courage to change the things I can, and the wisdom to know the difference. Amen.

—*Reinhold Niebuhr*

And behold, the star that they had seen at its rising preceded them, until it came and stopped over the place where the child was. They were overjoyed at seeing the star, and on entering the house they saw the child with Mary his mother. They prostrated themselves and did him homage. Then they opened their treasures and offered him gifts of gold, frankincense, and myrrh.

Matthew 2: 9–11

January

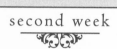

January 6 Epiphany

Meditation

In old European tradition, it was believed that decorations and greens hung for Christmas should not be taken down until Epiphany. The greens were thought to be imbued with spiritual qualities, and due to their connection to Christ's birthday, they should never be handled irreverently. It was considered very bad luck to simply toss out the decorations as we do today. Holly could either be burned or given to cattle to eat. Mistletoe sprigs were carefully preserved in the house to carry the blessings of this season throughout the coming year. Rosemary was often used to create scented water for washing skin, face, and hair. It was also put under beds to chase away bad dreams. This old tradition makes sense today, perhaps not because the greens have special powers, but because they are organic matter that can be rendered beneficial to the soil. Sprinkle pine needles under your rhododendrons and camellias; these plants love the acidic nature of the needles. The bare tree on its X-shaped stand is an ideal pea trellis, or it can be used as firewood or fed to a chipping machine to create valuable mulch. All else can go into the compost pile, where it will gradually decompose into rich humus.

Gardening

This month is for wading into the mound of gardening catalogs that has been building over the holidays. Browsing catalogs can be not only entertaining but also quite informative. While it rains or snows outside you can dive into a vicarious world of flowers in the dead of winter.

But approach these catalogs as you would any commercial. The vividly colored pictures of perfect plants in full bloom are eye-popping, but there is no guarantee that those plants will perform as well for you. The reality is that many of the plants shown require optimal conditions to look that good, if they even survive in your climate zone! There is nothing more important than doing your homework before you buy. You may be surprised to find that you can buy the same plant locally, for less money, and at three times the size of a mail-order bare root. Use catalogs for inspiration and to learn about and obtain plants you can't get locally. There is no question that your plant will be less stressed if it is handled by nursery workers rather than subjected to the sometimes rough handling of an air shipper.

PLANT

Winter Daphne

Daphne odora 'Aureo-marginata'

The little winter daphne has long been underestimated, but had the wise men known of its fragrance they would surely have brought flowers to the Christ child. This species is a native of China, where it was in cultivation by the year 1000. It was said to have been discovered by a Buddhist monk who fell asleep under a cliff and dreamed of delicate fragrance. When he awoke he still smelled the scent and followed it to its source, finding a plant he named sleeping scent. It was surely grown in temple grounds ever after, for the Chinese believe that fragrances, like the burned incense of the magi, rise up to heaven lighter than air.

Daphne was introduced into England in 1771, and so delicate does it appear that it was first grown in a heated greenhouse at Kew Gardens, then a cool greenhouse, then moved outdoors permanently. It's not a showy plant by any means, but the clusters of small, pale pink flowers emit incredible fragrance equal to gardenia or jasmine. It is called winter daphne because in mild climates, as in Kew's heated greenhouse, it will flower from January to March. Plants prefer surprisingly dry conditions during the summer, and overwatering in heavy soils is often the cause of their demise. They are beautiful candidates for sheltered sunny spots in small gardens protected from hot afternoon sun. This cultivar bears narrow gold margins on its green leaves, which contrast well against darker shade-garden plants. It is also believed to be even more cold hardy than the species.

Vision quickens the sight and warms the blood. He who makes a garden must have vision. He wonders.

Alfred Carl Hottes, *Garden Facts and Fancies*, 1949

Winter Daphne

Daphne odora 'Aureo-marginata'

Zone 7

Type: Evergreen shrub

Origin: China

Habitat: Part shade with well-drained soil

Size: 3 to 4 feet tall and as wide

Plant: Anytime, from containers

Notable feature: Fragrant flowers

Two of the three gifts of the magi were resins of woody plants native to Ethiopia. Frankincense is from *Boswellia carterii* and myrrh from *Commiphora myrrha*. The trunks of these trees were scored, causing a sticky resin to ooze out. After this resin dried rock hard, it was collected. These resins were central to the ancient perfume trade and to Egyptian mummification rites. Frankincense is still burned during the masses and rites of the Roman Catholic and Orthodox Churches.

Lord, you created flowers with fragrances that give us great pleasure in our gardens. You recognize these scents as fitting tribute, and let me never again inhale the perfume of lilac or rose without thinking of you. Amen.

Attiret's Chinoiserie

Until the eighteenth century, European gardens were painfully formal, with plants forcefully clipped into rigid geometric shapes. From the French parterre to the English knot garden, this rigidity may never have yielded to the naturalistic landscape style if it weren't for one Jesuit missionary.

Though many an English gardener will disagree, the naturalistic landscape style was not born in Europe but in the natural rock and water gardens of Chinese emperors. Collectively called chinoiserie by the French, the Asian style caught on and became popular, breaking landscaping out of rigid formality in layout, materials, and even garden architecture. If you follow the trail back far enough you realize that it began with one Jesuit missionary—Jean-Denis Attiret, a French priest well trained in fine painting and skilled in the decorative arts.

In 1737 Attiret was sent to China, where his work was admired by the emperor, who made the Jesuit his official artist. A letter from Attiret entitled "The Garden of Perfect Brightness" was published in Paris in 1749. It described the extensive grounds and gardens of Yüan-Ming Yüan known as the Old Summer Palace outside Beijing. This letter evoked the imaginations of French garden makers, whetting their appetite for pictures of these imaginative landscapes. Over many years Attiret painted hundreds of portraits and Chinese landscapes, both wild and cultivated, on glass and silk. His work would forever change the face of gardens in the West. He and three other Jesuits created sixteen tableaux in 1774 depicting China's victory over the Tatars. These were engraved in France for reproduction, but unfortunately Attiret did not live to see the result.

Then God said, "Let the earth bring forth vegetation: every kind of plant that bears seed and every kind of fruit tree on earth that bears fruit with its seed in it." And so it happened: the earth brought forth every kind of plant that bears seed and every kind of fruit tree on earth that bears fruit with its seed in it. God saw how good it was.

GENESIS 1:11–12

January

Meditation

God blessed the earth with an incredibly large kingdom of plants. The diversity is mind-boggling. Consider the range of sizes, for example. Compare the enormous hardwoods and creepers of the Amazonian rain forest and the flat, ground-hugging tundra plants that feed reindeer herds of the far north. The seasoned horticulturist is completely taken by this diversity, realizing that it is our treasured natural inheritance. While most people will rarely glimpse the whole universe of plants and its complexity, nevertheless, it is there for our discovery. As a gardener you have the ability to begin to understand the plant kingdom as a whole by studying the kinship of plants that share the same family, genus, or species. Begin with the pea family and learn to recognize the uniquely shaped flowers that bind its members. Study the cones of pine trees and see how they differ from the firs or cedars. Each bit of knowledge you accumulate will add to the giant puzzle, and after a while, you will come to appreciate the full beauty and intricacy of the natural world.

Next to the beauty of plants the thing that impresses us most is their endless variety—
so many kinds, no two exactly alike. How are we to explain these facts? At one time
the majority of those who gave any thought at all to the subject accepted the
explanation that the different kinds of plants and animals were "in the beginning"
created as they are with all their bewildering diversity. God spoke, and it was so.

C. Stuart Gager, *The Plant World*, 1931

Gardening

Large-scale pruning is best done in the winter months during the dormant season. Removing a tree, limbing an overgrown one, or hard pruning your aging shrubs is much easier when plants are barren. Provided the snow is not deep, get out the chain saw and pruning tools and bundle up to go out and prune away. A word of caution: While you won't have to fight the leaves in the wintertime, you will also not be able to tell the difference between living twigs and dead ones.

In the warmer regions, this is the month of winter rose pruning. In climates such as Florida or California, there is little need for hard pruning because roses do not become fully dormant. Simply cut off any twigs smaller than a pencil in diameter.

No matter where you live it's important to remove any canes that have died or are old and unproductive. Doing so forces more growth energy into producing new canes from right above the graft union. In the years to come, these new canes will become the main growing structure of your plant. You should also cut out any conflicting canes, or those that rub together, because the injuries to the canes that result from this rubbing will provide an entry for pests and diseases. Finally, when choosing which canes to prune, try to eliminate those buds that are growing toward the center of the plant, preserving those growing outward. This will encourage the rose to develop with a circle of canes around an open center, which will provide valuable air circulation that discourages disease such as mildew or black spot.

Important! Do not prune the old rose varieties that bloom but once in spring, or you will sacrifice all the flower-bearing stems and have no bloom at all that year! Prune these roses after they finish blooming in early summer.

Father Hugo's Rose

Rosa hugonis

Botanical reference works call it the Golden Rose of China, and it has become one of the most important of all the Asian roses. In the wilds of western China, an obscure missionary priest from Great Britain dedicated his life to God and the church. Known affectionately as Father Hugo, he served his mission family and became enamored of the beautiful flowering plants that grew all around him, in nature and in the Chinese gardens. He found the rare yellow flowering briar rose most captivating, for it reminded him of the little briar roses in the hedgerows of Britain. Realizing the value of a rare yellow rose, he collected seed in 1895 and sent it to the great center of horticulture, the Royal Botanic Gardens at Kew, England.

The new rose seedlings grown at Kew would revolutionize coloring among European species, introducing orange and the full range of golden yellow into our hybrid teas. The botanist W. Botting Helmsley described and classified the new rose species, then in 1905, to honor the little-known priest, he named the new species *Rosa hugonis*. By 1908, plants reached the Arnold Arboretum of Harvard University. By 1925, the species had won a number of awards.

Few modern roses exist that do not share at least some of their ancestry with Father Hugo's rose. It remains in cultivation and may be obtained bare root by special order through virtually any garden center or old-rose dealer. Although it is regrettable that we know little else of Father Hugo, his name is forever enshrined in the annals of the rose world.

Father Hugo's Rose

Rosa hugonis

Zone 4

Type: Large shrub rose

Origin: China

Habitat: Full sun and good soil

Size: Arching to 6 feet tall and as wide

Plant: Spring or fall, bare root or from containers

Notable feature: Fragrant, golden yellow flowers

 Lord, I thank you for blessing my life with so many different plants to discover. You assure me that no matter how long I live I shall never run out of discoveries. Help me to learn more about your creations so that I might come to know you better through them. Amen

Then, dismissing the crowds, he went into the house. His disciples approached him and said, "Explain to us the parable of the weeds in the field." He said in reply, "He who sows good seed is the Son of Man, the field is the world, the good seed the children of the kingdom. The weeds are the children of the evil one, and the enemy who sows them is the devil. The harvest is the end of the age, and the harvesters are angels. Just as weeds are collected and burned [up] with fire, so will it be at the end of the age."

MATTHEW 13:36–40

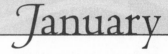

January

fourth week

Meditation

It is remarkable how easily influenced we are by the materialistic images all around us. Emaciated women have become our idols, yet no supermodel could turn more than a single spadeful of dirt. White sneakers are the leisure uniform, but we all know what they look like after five minutes in the garden. The messages we receive from our culture seek to tear us away from the garden, from our own spiritual Eden, with lures of material wealth and glamour. In fact, when we renew our baptismal vows we are asked, "Do you reject the glamour of sin?" Sin is glamorous just as many weeds grow into tall, mighty stalks that offer us nothing of value, and if allowed to mature they eventually take over the entire landscape with their unwanted progeny. Though we may find success in the material world, we should all strive to temper its ill effects with a thorough grounding in the garden.

Gardening

If you watch a farm laborer work magic with the common hoe, you invariably find a flat file nearby. At regular intervals the laborer pauses to run the file across the chiseled blade of the hoe, making it as sharp as possible. The sharper the blade, the less effort it will take to get the job done. Most home gardeners never give a thought to sharpening the hoe and may spend years hacking away with a dull, rounded blade edge. Approach a pruning task with dulled hand clippers and you'll end up with a sore arm. Your cuts will also tend to be ragged or torn, which makes it more difficult for the plant to heal.

Don't wait until you're in full spring-gardening mode to take care of your tools. Have all your pruning tools professionally sharpened and you'll be amazed at how easy the tasks become. Buy a flat file and hone your hoe, shovel, and any other sharp-edged tool for maximum results, and then resharpen them periodically throughout the year. A common electric bench grinder for the shed or garage is a worthwhile investment because it can hone your large tools in minutes while the flat file is used for quick touch-ups out in the garden. Replace any cracked or weak wood handles with new ones, or switch to the strong, lightweight, fiberglass alternatives now on the market. The old-time gardener and farmer wouldn't dream of passing the winter without such maintenance, and neither should you.

PLANT

Star Magnolia

Magnolia stellata

This is a gorgeous small tree and is considered the most cold hardy of all magnolias imported from Asia. It is deciduous and blooms in early spring before it leafs out. The flowers measure to 4 inches across and are unique among the magnolias, with twelve to fifteen long, slender white petals that radiate from the center like points of a star. The whole tree will be covered with them in such snow-white purity that it may appear to glow iridescently under moonlight. It was introduced to the West around the middle of the nineteenth century. The extent of its hardiness may reach zone 4, but it is more reliable in zone 5. It will grow no larger than 20 feet tall, which makes it a perfectly sized treasured accent in small or urban gardens. This is an excellent addition to old-fashioned cottage or country gardens as well. The most reliable cultivar is 'Royal Star.'

Star Magnolia

Magnolia stellata

Zone 5

Type: Large shrub or small tree

Origin: Japan

Habitat: Full sun and good soil

Size: To 10 feet tall and as wide

Plant: Spring or fall, bare root or from containers

Notable feature: Spectacular white spring blossoms

Lord, help me to ignore the glamour of sin that is all around me. Let me recognize the bad plants while still seedlings, when they can be more easily plucked out. But if I do neglect to pull my weeds in a timely way, give me the strength to dig them out, root and all. Amen.

February

Sacred Lily

Narcissus tazetta

Zone 5

Type: Hardy spring bulb

Origin: Asia Minor

Habitat: Full sun and good drainage

Size: 12 to 18 inches tall and
12 inches wide

Plant: Fall, from dormant bulbs

Notable feature: Early fragrant
white flowers

Sacred Lily

Narcissus tazetta

Many scholars believe the "rose of Sharon" in the Song of Songs is actually *Narcissus tazetta*, a wildflower bulb native to the Holy Land. It grows abundantly on the plain of Sharon between Palestine and the Mediterranean and on the hills that surround Jerusalem. Brought into gardens by ancient Egyptians, these flowers even figure largely in Greek mythology. The spring bulbs in this very large genus are easily recognized by their trumpet-shaped flowers, some of which are intensely fragrant.

You are the salt of the earth. But if salt loses its taste, with what can it be seasoned? It is no longer good for anything but to be thrown out and trampled underfoot. You are the light of the world. A city set on a mountain cannot be hidden. Nor do they light a lamp and then put it under a bushel basket; it is set on a lampstand, where it gives light to all in the house. Just so, your light must shine before others, that they may see your good deeds and glorify your heavenly Father.

MATTHEW 5:13–16

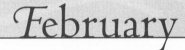

February

FEBRUARY 2 CANDLEMAS

Meditation

February is known for the appearance of the dreaded "false spring." This is a spate of abnormally warm weather that wreaks havoc with orchards. If the warmth lasts just long enough, the trees will begin to grow. Buds will swell and soon burst into flower. Inevitably the false spring is followed by a freeze or snowfall, which quickly kills the delicate flowers. The tree will not reflower that year, and the unfortunate orchard farmer will be left with no fruit and no income. Such fears surround February 2, the Feast of the Presentation of Our Lord, or Candlemas. If the sun shone through the clouds on this feast day, it was considered a sign from God that the coming growing season would produce a good crop.

The sun shines equally both on cedars and on every tiny flower. In just the same way,
God looks after every soul as if it had no equal. All is planned for the good
of every soul, exactly as the seasons are so arranged that the humblest daisy blossoms
at the appointed time.

St. Thérèse of Lisieux, *The Story of a Soul,* translated by John Beevers, 1957

Gardening

For most gardeners, the false spring is a perfect time to go out in the sunshine and catch up on dormant-season tasks. If trees have broken limbs from storms or heavy snow, cut the limbs off cleanly and seal the tree stub with household latex paint that matches the bark. If the wound is left unsealed, moisture can escape and cause unsightly dieback in the area surrounding it. Another area of concern is heaving soils caused by repeated freeze and thaw. Heaving soils can push bulbs and small plants upward, leaving their roots exposed. If plants or bulbs have been heaved up, press them gently back down into the soil. Then cover with mulch to protect from further heaving.

This is also the time of year to begin organizing for the summer garden. Gather the pots, six-packs, and flats you will need to grow your seedlings indoors on a sunny windowsill. Wash the containers thoroughly. Don't hesitate to run them through one or two dishwasher cycles to reduce the eggs, spores, and bacteria embedded in the containers from previous use. Be sure to buy sterile, disease-free, seed-starting medium to prevent any problems with damping-off and other diseases that afflict young seedlings.

Get ready to start cool-season seedlings that thrive in brisk weather of early spring. These first crops, such as cabbage, can often be planted outside by March or April in warmer regions, and by that time, the seedlings should be well along. When you put your early crops out, start second-crop seedlings indoors. These later crops include tomatoes and peppers, which should not be planted outside until the threat of frost has passed and soils are thoroughly warm.

PLANT

Snowdrop

Galanthus nivalis

It was once widely known as the "flower of the purification," or Candlemas bells, because legend says it was in bloom when Mary took her infant Jesus to the temple at Jerusalem. You might think of this as mere folklore until you look more closely at the origin of this lovely little bulb. It is native to Europe but species also grow in the Middle East and may have been well known in Israel in biblical times under the old Greek name, milk flower.

Snowdrops perform very well under the canopies of trees, where few other bulbs survive. They will persist and spread, naturalizing easily where conditions are right. Snowdrops are always welcome as the first flowers of the year and are named both for their white coloring and their ability to flower in the snow.

Snowdrop

Galanthus nivalis

Zone 7

Type: Hardy spring bulb

Origin: Europe

Habitat: Woodland, shade or part shade

Size: About 12 inches tall and as wide

Plant: Fall, from dormant bulbs

Notable feature: Unusual white flowers

 Lord, you are the light that shines on my world just as the sun shines on my garden. Bring peace, vigorous growth, and abundance to both life and garden, and protect us from unseasonable weather. Amen.

*I*f Candlemas Day be fair and bright—winter will have another flight;
If on Candlemas Day it be shower and rain—winter is gone and will not come again.
—Old English weather rhyme

In some areas of Europe, Candlemas was the last day that the plant remnants of holiday decorations could be burned and the ashes spread over the garden.

He took the blind man by the hand and led him outside the village. Putting spittle on his eyes he laid his hands on him and asked, "Do you see anything?" Looking up he replied, "I see people looking like trees and walking." Then he laid hands on his eyes a second time and he saw clearly; his sight was restored and he could see everything distinctly. Then he sent him home and said, "Do not even go into the village."

MARK 8:23–26

February

FEBRUARY 11 OUR LADY OF LOURDES

Meditation

We all need healing, whether it is physical, mental, or spiritual. When our infirmities become serious and medicine can no longer offer us any hope, we naturally look for miracles. Lourdes, France, is the undisputed center of miraculous healing in the Christian world, and the waters of this spring bring us hope that God will intervene in our suffering. The apparitions of our Blessed Mother, Mary, to a peasant girl, Bernadette, occurred in a natural outdoor setting at a plant-shrouded grotto, or shallow cave, in the countryside. As a sign, Mary caused a spring to appear, and the water that flows from it has wrought countless cures, over sixty of them recognized as miraculous by the church. But even though one who believes in the water may not be physically cured, there are healings of the mind and spirit that help us better cope with infirmity. A small fountain in the home or garden shrine allows us to cross ourselves each day with the water as a sign of our faith in God's miraculous healing powers. We don't need to travel to France to encounter Lourdes water, which is generously distributed free of charge by the Missionary Association of Mary Immaculate to anyone who asks. To obtain Lourdes water, simply submit your request at their Web site at www.oblatemissions.com.

While I was in prayer, the Lady said to me in a serious but friendly voice—"Go, drink and wash in the fountain." As I did not know where this fountain was, and as I did not think the matter important, I went towards the Gave [de Pau]. The lady called me back and signed to me with Her finger to go under the Grotto to the left, I obeyed but I did not see any water. Not knowing where to get it from, I scratched the earth and the water came. I let it get a little clear of the mud, then I drank and washed.... Unknown to the crowd, the Lady had pointed once more to the floor of the Grotto and told her little one, "Go, eat of the herbs you will find there."

Bernadette Soubrious, Lourdes, Ninth Apparition, February 25, 1858

Gardening

A pool and waterfall are at once the most challenging and most satisfying of all home-garden elements. Water adds a sense of animation to the landscape, and even a very small water feature can dramatically change the atmosphere of spaces that surround it. A water garden is simply an aquatic environment in which all sorts of wetland plants can be grown. Many gardeners keep fish in these gardens as well, from expensive koi to more affordable pond comets, which are actually just grown-up goldfish.

It is important that at the end of winter you give your water garden a spring cleaning to remove all of the accumulated organic matter, which can generate algae bloom in the warmer months to come. Drain the entire pool and scrub the liner gently to remove as much of the slimy algae as you can. If you must step into the pond to clean it, be sure to do this in bare feet to prevent damage to the pool's liner. Remove all the dead plant parts and any rocks or pebbles that have accumulated. Clean the pump and the entire filter system, including any hoses or pipes where strings of algae can build up, reducing capacity. Your water plants should be hosed off to remove accumulated algae on their leaf surfaces and pots. Any that have overgrown their containers, particularly reedlike marginals, can be divided into many new plants. Treat your water lilies to aquatic plant fertilizer pellets to stimulate growth and more bloom.

PLANT

English Lavender
Lavandula angustifolia

The rich scent of lavender, a shrub well known in Europe since before the Roman Empire, is always associated with cleansing and freshness. Its name is rooted in the Latin verb *lavo,* "to wash," because it was a favorite component in Roman baths. French lavender, *Lavandula dentata* 'Candicans,' and Spanish lavender, *Lavandula stoechas,* are the best choices for hot, dry Mediterranean-like climates. English lavender does better in cooler northern climates. The plants share aromatic green-gray foliage and make choice, small-garden shrubs. They provide useful flower spikes that hold up well when dried, hence their Marian name, Mary's drying plant. Lavender came to represent the virtues of purity and cleanliness and thus became associated with the chastity of Mary. Easy to grow and widely available, lavender may be cultivated in traditional terra-cotta pots that can be brought indoors to scent the house during cold northern winters. Use scissors to gently shear leaf tips to release the aromatic oils.

French Lavender

Lavandula dentata 'Candicans'

Zone 4

Type: Evergreen semiwoody perennial

Origin: Europe

Habitat: Full sun with good drainage

Size: To 3 feet tall and as wide

Plant: Anytime, from containers

Notable feature: Aromatic blue flowers for herbal crafts and foods

O my mother, in your heart I placed all the anguish of my heart, and it is there that I gain strength and courage.
—Petition, Grotto of Our Lady of Lourdes

At the time when the Lord God made the earth and the heavens—while as yet there was no field shrub on earth and no grass of the field had sprouted, for the Lord God had sent no rain upon the earth and there was no man to till the soil, but a stream was welling up out of the earth and was watering all the surface of the ground—the Lord God formed man out of the clay of the ground and blew into his nostrils the breath of life, and so man became a living being.

Genesis 2:4–7

February

Meditation

If you explore the creation stories of cultures around the world, in nearly all of them humans are first formed from one of two common sources: trees, the largest living things on earth, or the earth itself. If you think about it, primitive humans derived much of their material culture—their food, medicine, shelter, tools, and much more—primarily from plants. Since all plants came out of the soil, then human beings too must be similarly connected to this source of living plants. Our own creation story of Genesis, in which God formed Adam from clay, shares this same age-old connection to soil. The fact that the type of soil is indicated adds further credence, for wet clay is plastic, meaning that it can be molded into a particular shape and will stay that way. As gardeners, we also know that the concretelike hardness of dry clay is a lasting, impenetrable substance. We should celebrate the fact that each of us is a work of art intrinsically connected to our own garden soil.

*In the beginning God created the heaven and the earth. This is a statement
of tremendous reach, introducing the cosmos; for it sets forth in the fewest words
the elemental fact that the formation of the created earth lies above and before man,
and that therefore it is not man's but God's. Man finds himself upon it,
with many other creatures, all parts in some system which, since it is beyond man
and superior to him, is divine.*

Liberty Hyde Bailey, *The Holy Earth,* **1918**

Gardening

The foundation of organic gardening is the living soil. What may appear to be an inert material is actually a tiny universe of living organisms that exist within a structure of mineral grains and the residues of decomposing plants. The organisms are algae, fungi, and bacteria, which feed on organic matter to render it more beneficial to plant roots. Organic gardeners continually fortify their soils to provide plenty of food for the organisms so these populations remain high, and these organisms in turn make plants better able to resist pests and diseases. Newcomers to gardening think that you add your compost or manure and it remains in the soil indefinitely, but in reality it is consumed, sometimes in a matter of weeks or months. The secret to a productive garden is to add huge amounts of organic matter to the soil on a continual basis, and now is the time to start accumulating it for your spring garden. Bagged manure might be just fine for an average backyard, but be sure to check prices because they can vary drastically. If you're tending a large, organic vegetable garden, consider buying the manure in bulk, by the truckload or by the pallet. You'll need a place to store it, but in the long run this is far more convenient as you'll have no bags to dispose of. The alternative is making a few dozen trips to the home improvement store, stuffing the bags into the trunk and backseat of your car, and savoring the lingering aroma of manure whenever you take a drive!

PLANT

Crocus

Crocus vernus hybrids

The saffron listed with many other fragrant plants in the Song of Songs is a dyestuff derived from *Crocus sativus,* a species native to Greece and Asia

Minor. The only parts of the flower used were the stigma and style, which were plucked out of each individual flower, requiring four thousand flowers to yield an ounce of saffron. Our crocus bulbs are native to the Mediterranean from Spain eastward to Afghanistan. They have been cultivated in gardens since the Renaissance but did not catch on until the Victorians made it popular to force crocus bulbs indoors and plant masses of them in lawns. Our crocuses bloom so early they often pop up through snow-covered ground. Their small size is compensated for by their bloom season, a time when we are hungry for any color in the garden. Today's garden crocuses are divided into the early flowering "snow" crocuses, which are close to the original species, and the "Dutch" crocuses, which are modern hybrids that produce larger flowers and bloom a few weeks later than the snow crocuses. Combining both types in the garden extends the bloom display to well over a month. Crocuses are available in a variety of colors, including golden yellow, cream, purple, and lavender.

The holy earth is ever calling, but dull persons call it dirt.

Alfred Carl Hottes, *Garden Facts and Fancies,* **1949**

Crocus

Crocus vernus hybrids

Zone 4

Type: Spring bulb

Origin: Europe

Habitat: Full sun or part shade

Size: 6 inches tall and as wide

Plant: Fall, from dormant bulbs

Notable feature: Among earliest-blooming flowers

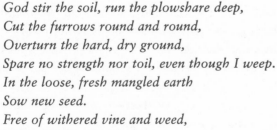

God stir the soil, run the plowshare deep,
Cut the furrows round and round,
Overturn the hard, dry ground,
Spare no strength nor toil, even though I weep.
In the loose, fresh mangled earth
Sow new seed.
Free of withered vine and weed,
Bring fair flowers to birth.
   —Prayer from Singapore, Church Missionary Society,
    Oxford Book of Prayer

The kingdom of heaven is like a landowner who went out at dawn to hire laborers for his vineyard. After agreeing with them for the usual daily wage, he sent them into his vineyard. Going out about nine o'clock, he saw others standing idle in the marketplace, and he said to them, "You too go into my vineyard, and I will give you what is just." So they went off. [And] he went out again around noon, and around three o'clock, and did likewise. Going out about five o'clock, he found others standing around, and said to them, "Why do you stand here idle all day?" They answered, "Because no one has hired us." He said to them, "You too go into my vineyard." When it was evening the owner of the vineyard said to his foreman, "Summon the laborers and give them their pay, beginning with the last and ending with the first."

MATTHEW 20:1–8

February

fourth week

Meditation

In our culture of luxury, the idea of physical labor is not celebrated. Yet at the heart of gardening lies the work, which transcends mere labor and elevates it to something more. If all the people who spent so much time at the gym used that work energy to cultivate the earth instead, there would be no shortage of food in the world and everyone would be healthier and richer for it.

This sanctity of labor is also the center of monastic life: while the body works, the mind is freed for contemplation. The Benedictine motto is To work is to pray; to pray is to work. This connection integrates spirituality into our hours of digging, pulling weeds, and watering and tending our plants. No one who believes it is better to sit or lie down than to work will ever create or truly enjoy a garden. An old gardener's proverb states it clearly: No garden was ever made by sitting in the shade. While our bodies may argue with sore knees or blistered fingers, at the end of the day we often look over the results to find a deep satisfaction and inner peace that is shared only by artisans, farmers, and missionaries.

*When God wanted sponges and oysters, He made them and put one on a rock and the
other in the mud. When He made man, He did not make him to be a sponge or an
oyster; He made him with feet, and hands, and head, and heart, and vital blood,
and a place to use them, and said to him, "Go work!"*

Henry Ward Beecher, *Royal Truths*, 1866

Gardening

Most gardeners nurse a love-hate relationship with their lawn mowers. We
love our mower because it turns shaggy turf into a beautiful, green carpet
each time we mow. We hate the mower when it won't start or cut evenly
and because it is a burden to push across the grass. All these things we hate
about the mower are rooted in simple maintenance or, more specifically,
the lack of it.

Lawn mowers aren't cheap, so it pays to take good care of your mower.
First, *keep the mower clean.* Wash the mower off with the hose after each
use so the clumps of clippings do not dry out and harden under the mower
deck, which can put undue strain on the drive mechanism and make changing the blade difficult. *Keep the mower blade sharp.* Dull mower blades will
produce a ragged cut, particularly in wet conditions when the grass is very
long or is flowering. It's a good idea to have two blades, one on the mower
and the other well sharpened for a quick switch, so that you aren't forced
to hike to get it sharpened before you can finish a mowing job. *Keep the
spark plug clean.* A carbon-fouled spark plug is the most common reason
for hard starting, particularly after a mower has been sitting awhile.
Remove the plug, and if it's black, gently clean it with a small wire brush.
Then, replace the spark plug and start up the mower.

Butterfly Bush
Buddleia davidii

This rangy, fast-growing shrub was named for its relationship to butterflies. The flowers are nectar rich, and many types of butterfly can be seen hovering around plants whenever they are in bloom. This plant was discovered about 1857 by Armand David, a missionary Jesuit working in China, and the species name commemorates his find. These shrubs reach a startling size in just one growing season and will reach up to eight feet at maturity. The branches are topped with large cone-shaped flowers in shades of purple, pink, or white, depending on the variety. Dwarf forms make the butterfly bush practical for smaller gardens. The buddleia is hardy to zone 5, where the plants will die back by degrees and defoliate with the first frost. In spring, cut away all the dead twigs and branches and new top growth will soon flesh it out again. This is a reliable, easy-to-grow, cottage-garden-style plant favored in habitat gardens. It is also perfect in the traditional garden for filling out beds and borders with large, bushy background foliage and flowers that bloom all summer.

Occupation was one of the pleasures of Paradise, and we cannot be happy without it.

Anna Brownwell Jameson, 1794–1860

Butterfly Bush

Buddleia davidii

Zone 5

Type: Deciduous flowering shrub

Origin: China

Habitat: Full sun

Size: 6 to 8 feet tall and 4 to 6 feet wide

Plant: Fall or spring, from containers

Notable feature: Attracts butterflies

 Lord, when I am tempted to sit rather than work in my garden, remind me that I am never at peace after sitting . . . only after gardening. Amen.

ARMAND'S DOVE

All the sciences concerned with the works of creation increase the glory of their Author. They are praiseworthy in themselves and holy in their objective, for to know the truth is to know God.

ARMAND DAVID, *ABBÈ DAVID'S DIARY*, 1949

Sometime around the mid-nineteenth century, a French Jesuit missionary arrived in Peking and prepared to journey inland. Young Armand David had spent his youth studying the natural sciences and was well trained in both botany and zoology. He would make three expeditions that were so successful he was provided special freedom and funding from the National Museum of Natural History in Paris. But it was the second trip into eastern Tibet, from 1868 to 1870, that proved a botanic treasure trove. His reports describe a rhododendron with trunks one foot in diameter. That trip yielded a staggering 1,500 species of plants formerly unknown in the West. These included the extraordinary dove tree, later named after him as *Davidia involucrata*. David's collections, which were forwarded to the museum, likely fell into the hands of Adrien Renè Franchet at the Jardin des Plantes, the center of French botany. David is credited with discovery of the following plants, many of which were named for him: mountain peach, *Prunus davidiana;* the ground cotoneaster, *Cotoneaster perpusillus; Rhododendron davidii;* and ten other new species. Although his name is honored in the species of butterfly bush *Buddleia davidii,* it was actually another French missionary, Jean Andre Soulie, who sent the first seed of that plant to Europe.

Ash Wednesday

By the sweat of your face
　　　shall you get bread to eat,
Until you return to the ground,
　　　from which you were taken;
For you are dirt,
　　　and to dirt you shall return.

GENESIS 3:19

Meditation

For gardeners this is the most appropriate of all Catholic traditions because it is rooted in the idea that our bodies are of the earth and in burial we return to it. In fact, it was even more profound in the days before iron caskets and concrete vault graves. The natural decomposition that is the fate of all organic matter ensures that when our soul is freed, our body will become one with the earth. When a tree is planted on a grave (a common practice until recently), this natural process is made visible as our bodies provide nourishment for a beautiful living thing. Unfortunately modern burial practices have separated us from this cycle.

The anointing with ashes is a sign of penance and sorrow for our sins. It is rooted in the pre-Christian agricultural rites of Europe, when the fields were burned to remove the last of the previous year's crops and to destroy overwintering pests that threatened the new sprouts. It is in this season that the ancient druids set their new year, for it is both the end and the beginning. Thus we anoint ourselves with the ashes of plants, signifying the purging of the previous year's season of sin and our beginning of the process of spiritual rebirth.

It may seem an irreverent thought to some, but it is unarguable that
a churchyard is richer in good fertilizer than a garden full of modern chemicals,
and in town and city churchyards, selective weed killers have to be used to suppress
the rampant growth fueled by bonemeal.

Brian J. Bailey, *Churchyards of England and Wales,* **1987**

Gardening

Phosphorous is one of the three major nutrients found in most fertilizer and on the label is the middle number of the formula. For example, a fertilizer listed as 10-15-7 contains 15 percent phosphorus. Phosphorus is vital for healthy plants, stimulating both root and fruit production. Young seedlings planted in spring need adequate phosphorus in the soil if they are to develop a strong root system. When the time comes for vegetables to flower and set fruit, this nutrient is of equal value.

Bonemeal is the oldest known source of phosphorus fertilizer. It is about 30 percent phosphorus, but only about 4 percent of that is available to plants, or can be used by them. Bonemeal was replaced in the twentieth century by the more potent chemical form, superphosphate of lime 0-25-0, some forms of which make 40 to 50 percent of the phosphate available to plants. Organic gardeners generally prefer bonemeal as a more natural source of phosphate, and bonemeal has once more become widely available for use in chemical-free kitchen gardens. See Peaceful Valley Farm Supply in the resources section at the back of this book for sources of bonemeal and other organic fertilizers.

PLANT

English Yew

Taxus baccata

English churchyards often contain one or more yew trees, which are needled evergreens native to Europe. These are considered the oldest trees in Britain, with some dating back to the Norman Conquest in 1066. They are present in these places of burial because yew is very poisonous and the yards were fenced off from browsing livestock. The trees are also the source of wood for the English longbow. *Taxus baccata* is an excellent vertical evergreen that requires little care and grows in almost any soil. It is valued as a more cold-hardy alternative to the Italian cypress. English yew offers a great-looking, formal columnar shape that will tolerate shaping for a more geometric appearance.

English Yew

Taxus baccata

Zone 5

Type: Needled evergreen tree

Origin: Asia Minor

Habitat: Full sun

Size: To 60 feet tall and 20 feet wide

Plant: Anytime, from containers

Notable feature: Toxic to people and animals

Lord, all organic living things come back to the earth in the end. As my soul flies to you upon death, let my body decompose naturally, returning to the soil a small portion of what I have taken from it during my life. Amen.

March

Carnation

Dianthus caryophyllus

Zone 5

Type: Perennial

Origin: Europe

Habitat: Full sun

Size: 18 to 24 inches tall and as wide

Plant: Spring or fall, from containers

Carnation

Dianthus caryophyllus

The common name for this well-known flower is from the Latin word for flesh, *carnis,* as the flowers were originally a shade of pink likened to that of human flesh. Thus the carnation became associated with Jesus as the Word made flesh. The great artists of the Renaissance often used carnations symbolically in their paintings. One legend states that wherever Mary's tears fell upon the road to Calvary, a carnation grew as a symbol of motherly love. The flower later came to represent fidelity in marriage and carnal love.

Then the Lord God planted a garden in Eden, in the east, and he placed there the man whom he had formed. Out of the ground the Lord God made various trees grow that were delightful to look at and good for food, with the tree of life in the middle of the garden and the tree of the knowledge of good and bad.

A river rises in Eden to water the garden; beyond there it divides and becomes four branches.

Genesis 2:8–10

March

First Sunday of Lent
March 1 St. David's Day

Meditation

That mankind was created in a garden lends a special significance to the Genesis story for gardeners. It tells us that God chose an environment of plants as the most ideal place for humanity to dwell. He did not build a grand cathedral or mansions for us, nor did he place us in a cave. God chose a garden, a living vegetable kingdom in all its beauty and abundance.

As growers of plants we share in this legacy and honor it by becoming more familiar with creation through gardening. We come to know plants by name; we discover their relationships to one another and learn how to provide for their specific needs. In so doing, we glimpse the wonder of Eden, where the very same plants were created by the hand of God to surround Adam and Eve with a living, breathing paradise.

That there is no place more pleasant than a garden, may appear from God himselfe, who after he made Man, planted the Garden of Eden, and put him therein, that he might contemplate the many wonderful Ornaments wherewith Omnipotency had bedecked his Mother Earth. It was not so much for Adam's recreation, who at the time was not acquainted with wearinesse, as it was for his Instruction, but to us it will serve for both. There is not a Plant which growes but carries along with it the legible Characters of a Deity.

William Coles, *The Art of Simpling,* **1656**

Gardening

March is notorious for coming in like a lion, with fluctuating temperatures and tempestuous winds. Those warmer winds will begin to thaw or dry out rain-soaked soils, tempting us to begin tilling and working the soil. On a nice warm Saturday, we itch to get out into the garden, but sometimes the soil is not ready.

When you walk around on wet clay soils, the earth can easily become overly compacted and then dry in a compressed, bricklike state. It is devilishly difficult to repair such compaction later on. Tilling too early in any soil may also cause problems. It will destroy the natural structure of your soil, leaving it in an uncohesive granular state. Do not succumb to the almost irresistable temptation to plant. At this time of year it is wise to practice restraint and simply pull new weed sprouts.

A traditional bit of gardening wisdom goes like this: Upon St. David's Day, put oats and barley in the clay. Saint David isn't well known in America, but he is the patron saint of Wales. He is associated with the leek, a vegetable relative of the onion, and the Welsh wear leeks pinned to their hats on this day to honor David and celebrate the victory over Saxon invaders in 640.

PLANT

Common Hyacinth

Hyacinthus orientalis

These easy bulbs are treasured for their rich, intensely fragrant flowers. The stiff and waxy blossom spikes make hyacinths an excellent and long-lasting cut flower. Hyacinths originated in Turkey and throughout Asia Minor. Long beloved by the Persians, hyacinths did not reach the West until the sixteenth century. Just one hundred years later, more than two hundred varieties existed. Hyacinths are easy to force for indoor bloom and were popular in Victorian gardens for mass outdoor bedding displays. Unfortunately, tastes change, and the prominence of hyacinths has faded in modern times. Many of the old varieties have disappeared.

The hyacinth grows best outdoors in zones 5 to 7, but with protection, they will survive winter if well mulched in zone 4. Most hyacinths today are descended from *Hyacinthus orientalis,* often called Dutch hybrids, which thrive in a colder climate. The rare Roman hyacinth is far more tender but thrives in southern states that lack sufficient winter chilling for the Dutch hybrids to be sufficiently long-lived. You can plant modern hyacinths or help keep the old varieties alive by planting heirlooms from Old House Gardens bulb catalog, listed in the resources section of this book.

Common Hyacinth

Hyacinthus orientalis

Zone 5

Type: Hardy spring bulb

Origin: Asia Minor

Habitat: Full sun or part shade

Size: 8 to 14 inches tall and 12 inches wide

Plant: Fall, from dormant bulbs

Notable feature: Large fragrant flowers

Lord, may the warm winds of spring dry my garden soil so that I may begin turning the earth. Please prepare my spirit with your invisible winds of renewal during this time of Lent so that my spirit may also be reborn with the resurrected Christ at Easter. Amen.

May he live as long as the sun endures,
    like the moon, through all generations.
May he be like rain coming down upon the fields,
    like showers watering the earth,
That abundance may flourish in his days,
    great bounty, till the moon be no more.

PSALM 72:5–7

Meditation

Jesus was transfigured on a mountaintop before just three apostles: Peter, James, and John. It did not occur in a populated area but in a place human beings have gone since the earliest times to find quiet contemplation—it is a place of separation that seems more sky than earth. In the mountains we may see the stars more clearly, unencumbered by city lights, just as the first human beings witnessed them. Mountains thrust us into the sky, the heavenly realm from which sunlight and rain fall—the two essential natural elements that enable gardens and planted fields to flourish.

This Lenten season of the soul is a time when we should get away into the wilderness for just a day before the heavy work of the garden begins. Seek inspiration for your landscape in the models so perfectly wrought in nature.

Gardening

The rock garden evolved in the brutally harsh mountain highlands. Poor soils, extreme temperatures, and persistent dry winds forced plants to evolve into a low, ground-hugging profile. The charm of these natural miniature gardens amid the rocky crags was not lost on gardeners, who have long sought to recreate the windswept mountain-wildflower landscapes of the Alps in their home gardens. The tiny alpine plants give no hint of the invisible taproot that ventures deep into rock fissures, anchoring the plants to the mountainside and providing crucial access to moisture trapped deep in the rocks, far from the impossibly dry surface. With creative stonework, any natural or man-made slope can be rendered into a rock garden with high-altitude shrubs and wildflowers that will grow and bloom before anything else in the garden. While more heat-loving plants are thriving in the summer, alpines will have ceased their great reproductive efforts, fortifying themselves to withstand the next onslaught of winter.

PLANT

Rocky Mountain Beardtongue

Penstemon strictus

Penstemon are North American wildflowers, mostly perennial, which produce very showy wands of tubular flowers. A large number of species are native to North America in upper elevations of the Sierra Nevada, the Cascades, and the Rocky Mountains. This species ranges from Wyoming to New Mexico, attesting to its cold hardiness, and is found growing in rocky areas with very fast-draining, gravel-rich soils. Vivid lavender blossoms on plants nearly three feet tall are valued

God's wisdom is one, but it reveals itself in various forms; as, for instance, the sun is one but its rays show in various colors when they go through a prism.

Bahyah ibn Pakuda, *The Duties of the Heart*, eleventh century

in perennial borders and native plant gardens. Its striking visual quality, ease of cultivation, drought resistance, and longevity make *Penstemon* an outstanding candidate for Western landscapes where dry climate and infertile soils preclude heavier-feeding perennials.

Rocky Mountain Beardtongue

Penstemon strictus

Zone 4

Type: Hardy perennial

Origin: Rocky Mountain states

Habitat: Full sun

Size: 18 inches tall and as wide, 30 inches tall in bloom

Plant: Fall or spring, from containers

Lord, although I may not be able to climb mountains and touch the stars at night, allow me to discover that same mysterious beauty in my garden. Remind me to go out under a full moon and let the sounds of my neighbors fade away into silence, for only then will I find your majesty right here in the midst of my own backyard. Amen.

Meanwhile Moses was tending the flock of his father-in-law Jethro, the priest of Midian. Leading the flock across the desert, he came to Horeb, the mountain of God. There an angel of the LORD appeared to him in fire flaming out of a bush. As he looked on, he was surprised to see that the bush, though on fire, was not consumed. So Moses decided, "I must go over to look at this remarkable sight, and see why the bush is not burned."

When the Lord saw him coming over to look at it more closely, God called out to him from the bush, "Moses! Moses!" He answered, "Here I am." God said, "Come no nearer! Remove the sandals from your feet, for the place where you stand is holy ground."

EXODUS 3:1–5

March

MARCH 17 FEAST OF ST. PATRICK

There is much Irish gardening lore that surrounds St. Patrick's Day. Patrick stood as the great apostle of Christianity who converted the druids, who worshipped earth spirits that they believed dwelled in oak trees. Patrick earned his association with the shamrock after using its three-part leaf to illustrate the Holy Trinity.

Meditation

The story of the burning bush illustrates how God uses natural things to communicate with us. Certainly our gardens do not contain burning bushes, but many a seasoned gardener will agree that some shrubs speak in the silent language of plants. They display their needs in subtle signs of leaf, flower, and growth. As gardeners we must learn to read these subtle signs in order to know how to best tend our plants. It requires us to pause and inspect each part of the plant for clues to its condition, rather than view it as a mass of foliage or flowers. This is God speaking silently to gardeners, using a language that is uttered through his creations. Once we become open to the silent messages, they become all too insistent and the meaning perfectly clear.

Gardening

The date of the feast of St. Patrick marks the planting of peas in Britain and is about the time that gardeners in the southern states begin planting. Like Patrick's clover, peas are members of the legume clan. They prefer cooler weather and, in warm climates, tend to wither with the onset of summer heat. Gardeners too often plant peas when they plant tomatoes or corn, but peas mature much earlier and should be planted earlier. You can get up to 25 percent more productivity from your peas, be they snap peas, flat snow peas, or shell peas, by planting them along with an organic mycorrhizal inoculum that you can buy from most seed catalogs or garden centers. Simply sprinkle the granules over your seed before covering.

When you buy pea seeds this year, choose edible-pod types for a more diverse culinary experience. Chinese snow peas, with their flat pods, are essential in stir-fry. For small gardens, plant the dwarf varieties that fit much better into a spatially challenged yard. The new snap peas bear smaller sugary pods that are great to eat fresh and uncooked for an abundant supply of vitamin-rich, chemical-free snacks.

PLANT

Burning Bush
Euonymus alata

This marvelous deciduous shrub is named for its fiery fall color, which early botanists likened to the burning bush seen by Moses on Mount Horeb. Its crimson-pink color is so vivid it is hard to believe that this plant requires so little care. Burning bush is very cold hardy, to zone 3, and well suited to the northern states. It is native to Japan and was both introduced and classified in 1860 by Philip von Siebold, physician to the Dutch East India Company. *E. alatus* is a large shrub that will grow to about six feet tall and as wide at maturity for a large, bold color display. Smaller gardens will do best to use the dwarf *E. alata* 'Compactus' rather than the original species.

Burning Bush

Euonymus alata

Zone 3

Type: Deciduous shrub

Origin: China and Japan

Habitat: Full sun

Size: 6 to 8 feet tall and as wide

Plant: Fall or spring, from containers

Notable feature: Brilliant fall foliage color

Lord, grant me a closeness to natural things that was so clearly felt by St. Patrick. Allow my relationship with you to be warmed by the bright sun, refreshed by a summer breeze, and made fertile by the brown earth beneath my feet. Amen.

The pious prune their roses on St. Patrick's Day,
The worldly on Grand National Day.

GREGOR AND THE PEAS

The very foundation of modern hereditary genetics was built on the lowly garden pea, *Pisum sativum,* and uncovered by a European Augustinian monk, Gregor Mendel. Gregor spent eight years in the greenhouse of the Monastery of St. Thomas, growing upward of ten thousand pea specimens. He inspected and recorded the attributes of each new plant to find patterns in the chain of inheritance. He looked at how specific traits such as flower color are distributed from one generation to the next. Mendel worked with thirty-four different kinds of peas to define three laws: dominance, segregation, and assortment. At first this revelation was not widely accepted among his peers. Only after Mendel's death in 1884 did the great scientists of modern genetics discover how profoundly important the monk's laws were to modern science. Even today the science of genetics remains rooted in this monk's groundbreaking work. More information can be found in Robin Marantz's recent book on Mendel's life and work written for a general audience, *The Monk in the Garden* (Henig, 2000).

And he spoke to them at length in parables, saying: "A sower went out to sow. And as he sowed, some seed fell on the path, and birds came and ate it up. Some fell on rocky ground, where it had little soil. It sprang up at once because the soil was not deep, and when the sun rose it was scorched, and it withered for lack of roots. Some seed fell among thorns, and the thorns grew up and choked it. But some seed fell on rich soil, and produced fruit, a hundred or sixty or thirtyfold."

MATTHEW 13:3–8

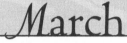

fourth week

MARCH 21 SPRING EQUINOX
MARCH 25 FEAST OF THE ANNUNCIATION

Meditation

The Feast of the Annunciation, the good news that Mary was miraculously with child, combines perfectly with the spring equinox to mark the beginning of the planting season. The church fathers no doubt sought to underscore the importance of the conception by placing the feast on this celestially auspicious occasion. The equinox and solstice dates were the chief hallmarks of planting and harvesting that ordered the early farmer's annual cycle. We as gardeners understand this connection far more deeply than many others, for whether it is life in the womb or the emergence of a seedling, all life is a miracle.

If there is any living thing which might explain to us the mystery beyond this life, it should be seeds. We pour them curiously into the palm, dark as mystery, brown or gray as earth, bright sometimes with scarlet of those beads worked into Buddhist rosaries. We shake them there, gazing, but there is no answer to this knocking on the door. They will not tell where their life has gone, or if it is there, any more than the lips of the dead.

Donald Culross Peattie, *Flowering Earth*, 1939

Gardening

The parable of the sower tells us much about the successful sowing of seeds. The seedbed, be it in the soul or the soil, is crucial to the survival of the seed. The rule of thumb is that all types of seed should be covered with a layer of soil twice the diameter of the seed itself. If you cover the seed with heavy soil, it presents a barrier to the new seedling, which now must work harder to break through. It's best to mix up a special batch of lightweight seed-covering soil to use in lieu of regular garden earth. To one part natural soil add an equal amount of the following, depending on what you have available: ground peat moss, sterilized steer manure, compost, or leaf mold. Then create your seed trench or depression in freshly tilled soil, sow the seed, and lightly cover with your mix to the proper depth. Press it down gently with your hand to prevent washout and lightly sprinkle with water. You will be very surprised at how quickly your seeds germinate and sprout when sown in this rich, soft seedbed.

PLANT

Kale

Brassica oleracea

Kale, an ancient member of the cabbage family, has been cultivated longer than any of its close kin, and some say it was so valued by the Celts that they were named after it. Kale became the vitamin-rich mainstay of the European monastic communities, where agricultural self-sufficiency was essential to guarding against deficiency diseases such as scurvy. Kale was in every garden to provide greens throughout the winter, and it actually tastes sweeter after a frost. The monks simply picked off the lower leaves as needed rather than uproot the whole plant as one would a cabbage. Kale leaves can be picked long before the plants mature, but with the onset of hot weather they are likely to bolt and flower. If flowers are cut off, the kale will begin producing leaves again in the fall, so don't be in a hurry to pull the plants out. These greens are delicious steamed or stewed in broth for flavor and to increase the vitamin content. Some of the most reliable varieties are improved dwarf Siberian, white Russian, and ultra cold-hardy winterbor. Colorful kales with purple-pink leaves include redbor and winter red.

Kale

Brassica oleracea

All zones

Type: Annual leaf vegetable

Origin: Europe

Habitat: Full sun, kitchen garden

Size: About 18 to 24 inches tall and as wide

Plant: From seed or six-packs

Notable feature: Edible leaves taste better in winter

Lord, just as I make a comfortable bed for the young seed, remind me to keep my heart and soul prepared for you at all times. Please soften it with love, enrich it with generosity, and let hope keep it open and ready to receive you. Amen.

April

Colorado Columbine

Aqueligia caerulea

Zone 3

Type: Biennial

Origin: Alpine slopes of the Rocky Mountains

Habitat: Sun in the northern United States, light shade in the South

Size: 18 to 30 inches tall and as wide

Plant: Spring, from seed or containers

Notable feature: Woodland garden color, replant every third year

Columbine

Aqueligia vulgaris

This has been the flower of the Holy Spirit since ancient times. The European species was first associated with the seven gifts of the Holy Spirit, as its flower spikes typically produced about seven flowers. It appears in many old religious paintings as a sign of the invisible presence of the Holy Spirit. Thus its name was derived from the Latin for "dove" or "dovelike," *columba*. Some observers even commented that the shape of the flower with its prominent spurs also suggested the birds.

I planted, Apollos watered, but God caused the growth. Therefore, neither the one who plants nor the one who waters is anything, but only God, who causes the growth. The one who plants and the one who waters are equal, and each will receive wages in proportion to his labor. For we are God's co-workers; you are God's field, God's building.

1 CORINTHIANS 3:6–9

April

APPROXIMATE LAETARE SUNDAY

Laetare Sunday, or the fourth Sunday of Lent, was once a joyful celebration of the catechumens who had proved themselves worthy to be baptized. The church was decorated for the occasion with fresh flowers under special dispensation from the Lenten ban. Another symbol of this Laetare Sunday is the golden rose carried by the pope after the Mass. Originally it had been a fresh rose, which represented Christ as the "flower sprung from the root of Jesse." Although neither event is still widely celebrated, in warm climates the earliest roses bloom, coinciding with the celebration of those preparing for their baptism.

Meditation

Perhaps one of the most profound aspects of gardening is the realization that we may till the soil, plant, and water, but only God makes the plants live and grow. To imagine that everyone who works the ground is God's coworker means that each of us becomes closer to God through even the most insignificant tasks. We tend to believe that we have much more control over our lives than we actually do, and it is only when we face the uncertain future that we learn to rely exclusively on God as the great overseer of humanity. We do have free will to plant our seeds and to water and feed them, but if God does not wish that seed to sprout, it will not grow and there's nothing we can do about it. Gardening teaches us to accept our disappointments and to celebrate our successes as a tribute to a very intimate cooperation between ourselves and God.

When we think of the origin of the Dahlia, how it started from a little flower not much larger than a ten-cent piece, single only, I appreciate the fact that the great Creator who made man in the likeness of his image to be copartner with him in creating some of the most beautiful and useful things in the world, and it developed his mind, I can really see why he did not put the soul into the flower. He put it into use, and we have expressed it in the development of just such beautiful flowers.

George Washington Carver, *George Washington Carver in His Own Words,*
edited by Gary R. Kremer, 1987

Gardening

The first flats of bedding flowers that come into the garden center are varieties that thrive in the cool weather of spring. The delicate Iceland poppies, *Papaver nudicaule,* are impossibly light and slender. The petite but rugged English primrose blooms vividly in small but intense bursts of color. The whole *Viola* clan offers a full painter's palette to work with. Many gardeners don't realize that these early flowers can survive a little cold snap without much damage. It's fine to begin planting them in pots that can be brought in on an unusually cold night. Use their bright color and living presence to celebrate each new soul to be presented to the church at the Easter Vigil. And as you plant them, know that God works with you as you brighten the world this spring.

PLANT

Heartsease
Viola tricolor

The ancestor of our common garden pansy is the native wild pansy of England, *Viola tricolor,* named for the three colors of its flower: blue, white, and yellow. Using this small wildflower, nineteenth-century plant breeders worked hand in hand with God to reveal the spectrum of traits hidden in the genes of the *Viola*. From this came garden violas in a broad range of colors and finally the mammoth flowers of the hybrid pansies, which exhibit a rainbow of vibrant colors. Yet that little flower of England known affectionately as Johnny-jump-up is still popular today and is often found growing beside its showier relatives. This spring, delve into the diversity of this single clan and discover just how much variation exists within the humble little species *Viola tricolor.*

You are privileged to create new varieties of roses, new shapes, new colors. To you it is granted to improve the garden of the Lord.

Pope Pius XII, 1955

Heartsease

Viola tricolor

All zones

Type: Spring annual flower

Origin: Europe

Habitat: Sun, part shade in hot climates

Plant: From seed or six-packs

Size: 6 to 10 inches tall and as wide

Notable feature: Edible flowers for salad or garnish

Lord, you have sequestered a microscopic universe within the genes of every one of your creations. Help me to realize that although they are invisible, these treasures are indeed part of your divine plan, and we are obliged to work with you to reveal them for the benefit of mankind. Though I may be afraid of the unfathomable world of genetics, fill me with courage and hope that within it lies an end to famine and disease on earth. Amen.

Then he proceeded to tell the people this parable. "[A] man planted a vineyard, leased it to tenant farmers, and then went on a journey for a long time. At harvest time he sent a servant to the tenant farmers to receive some of the produce of the vineyard. But they beat the servant and sent him away empty-handed. So he proceeded to send another servant, but him also they beat and insulted and sent away empty-handed. Then he proceeded to send a third, but this one too they wounded and threw out. The owner of the vineyard said, 'What shall I do? I shall send my beloved son; maybe they will respect him.' But when the tenant farmers saw him they said to one another, 'This is the heir. Let us kill him that the inheritance may become ours.' So they threw him out of the vineyard and killed him. What will the owner of the vineyard do to them? He will come and put those tenant farmers to death and turn over the vineyard to others."

LUKE 20:9–16

April

Meditation

As gardeners, we are all stewards of our land. That ground, whether it is acres of country estate or a tiny postage stamp in the middle of a large city, is temporarily on loan to us from God. We are granted the privilege of working it for him. Stewardship is more than merely planting that earth each year, for we have the opportunity to improve it on a far more lasting basis. For example, a flower or kitchen garden of seasonal plants will die out if no one is there to replant it each spring. But when you plant trees you contribute lasting values that benefit human beings for decades to come. Perhaps as gardeners it is our duty to do more than just plant for ourselves, but to invest in the future by planting to improve the living environment of our homes and, on a larger scale, that of our neighborhoods and communities.

Merely to make the earth productive and to keep it clean and to bear a reverent regard
for its products is the special prerogative of a good agriculture and a good citizenry
founded thereon; this may seem at the moment to be small and ineffective as against
mad impersonal and limitless havoc, but it carries the final healing; and while the land
worker will bear much of the burden on his back, he will also redeem the earth.

Liberty Hyde Bailey, *The Holy Earth,* **1918**

Gardening

In the North, April begins the short bare-root planting season when deciduous trees and some shrubs are sold freshly dug out of the earth. Despite
their low cost and sticklike appearance, bare-root trees tend to develop much
better root systems overall because they have not been forced to root in a
container. It is important to choose bare roots carefully and reject any with
nicks or gouges at the base of the trunk. Choose plants with more extensive
root systems and a preponderance of thin fibrous roots. Be sure to set the
tree at the same level in your yard as it was in the growing field, which is
shown by the change in bark color on the trunk. If you plant too deep the
bark will rot away and kill the tree in the first year. Eliminate drying air
pockets in the soil around the roots by packing the earth down evenly before
you water. The low cost of bare roots means you can afford to plant more
trees and shrubs that will permanently beautify your home landscape.

PLANT

Tulip Tree
Liriodendron tulipifera

If God ever made a perfect shade tree, it is this species. Ideally suited to home
landscapes, boulevards, and city parks, the tulip tree is native to the eastern
United States and is hardy to zone 4. Specimens are known to exceed two
hundred years of age, a long life ensured by the fact that the tree is free of
most problem pests or diseases. A well-behaved root system and the lack of
messy litter make it well suited to almost any situation. The large-lobed leaves
turn a clear, butter yellow in the fall. The name is derived from its unique
tuliplike yellow blossoms that bloom each year during the growing season,
but these appear more profusely on the upper part of the canopy. Although

slow growing in its early years, this tree compensates with its longevity and disease resistance. A healthy tulip tree will reach 120 feet at maturity with a canopy up to 75 feet in diameter. Plant from a bare root in fall or early spring for best results.

Tulip Tree

Liriodendron tulipifera

Zone 4

Type: Deciduous shade tree

Origin: Eastern United States

Habitat: Sun

Size: 50 feet tall and 30 feet wide

Plant: Spring or fall, bare root or from containers

Notable feature: Golden fall color

Lord, watch over the trees I plant so they will grow tall and flourish in the light of the sun. Let their spreading branches shade the hot pavement, and the leaves add oxygen to this city air. Please bring the birds to nest in the branches as an acknowledgment of my stewardship and my desire to make the world a better and more beautiful place, one tree at a time. Amen.

He taught them a lesson. "Consider the fig tree and all the other trees. When their buds burst open, you see for yourselves and know that summer is now near; in the same way, when you see these things happening, know that the kingdom of God is near."

LUKE 21:29–31

April

Meditation

We feel the onset of spring through a million silent messages that tell us change is at hand. Perhaps it is the position of the sun through our window or the length of shadows at noon. The new blades of grass or the swelling of tree buds speak the visual language of God uttered through signs in the garden. These changes are more profoundly visible in spring, for it is the most active of all seasons. When we were children, we moved too quickly through life, gauging our experiences in quantity rather than quality. Rare is the child who will pause to note that the cherry buds are swelling or that the tips of crocus now push up through the snow. One of the rewards of being more mature is that we cease that frenetic activity, which allows us to see and understand these subtle signs in nature. Best of all, we realize that each discovered sign is a treasure that makes us rejoice in this growing intimacy with the source of all life, God.

Gardening

Around this time each year, the early flowering shrubs begin to bloom. These are the cold-hardy, old-fashioned favorites that adorned our grandmothers' gardens and now brighten our own. When the yellow forsythia and coral-red quince explode into color, we know spring is at hand.

When plants become too large and overgrown or simply need to be shaped, you must prune them at the right time of year to ensure that not a spring will pass without flowers. By taking note of which twigs and branches produce the flowers, you'll discover the optimum season for pruning your flowing shrubs. If the blooms are only on the ends of the branches, you'll know that the plant produces flowers on twigs that grew the previous season. If you prune that new growth in winter, the plant will not bloom the following spring. If the flowers are distributed on the lower part of the plant, then you know that the plant flowers on the older wood. Any rangy top-growth on these plants should be pruned during the winter.

PLANT

Flowering Quince

Chaenomeles x superba

Plant flowering quince and God will tell you in bold coral-red when spring is nigh. The incredibly beautiful bare branches of the quince are quite striking both in the garden and as a cut flower. Large sprays of blooming quince are cut and placed in large porcelain vases to celebrate the Chinese new year. The *Chaenomeles* x *superba* group of hybrids that developed in the twentieth century combine the best of both Chinese and Japanese native quince species. The *superba* hybrids are universally cold hardy to zone 4 and thrive in practically all garden exposures except deep shade. They grow in all types of soil and can be surprisingly drought resistant. Under the right conditions, quinces produce a highly fragrant but inedible fruit that if brought indoors will perfume an entire room.

Flowering Quince

Chaenomeles x *superba*

Zone 4

Type: Deciduous flowering shrub

Origin: Hybrid of species from China and Japan

Habitat: Sun or part shade

Size: 3 to 6 feet tall and 4 to 8 feet wide

Plant: Spring or fall, from containers

Notable feature: Brilliant coral-red spring flowers

 Lord, as my garden awakens with the early signs of spring, grant me the courage to examine my conscience and to renew myself as well. Just as the garden begins anew each year, let my Easter confession separate me from the sins of my past so that I may grow and flourish too. Amen.

Centuries ago in Europe, parishioners swept out their church during Holy Week so that each person could carry some of the dust home to scatter in their garden. It was believed the sacred particles protected plants and increased fertility.

I will open up rivers on the bare heights,
>and fountains in the broad valleys;
I will turn the desert into a marshland,
>and the dry ground into springs of water.

I will plant in the desert the cedar,
>acacia, myrtle, and olive;
I will set in the wasteland the cypress,
>together with the plane tree and the pine,

That all may see and know,
>observe and understand,

That the hand of the Lord has done this.

ISAIAH 41:18–20

Holy Week

The Blessing of the Palms

On the next day, when the great crowd that had come to the feast heard that Jesus was coming to Jerusalem, they took palm branches and went out to meet him, and cried out:

>"Hosanna!
>Blessed is he who comes in the name of the Lord,
>>[even] the king of Israel."

JOHN 12:12–13

On the first day you shall gather foliage from majestic trees, branches of palms and boughs of myrtles and of valley poplars, and then for a week you shall make merry before the Lord, your God.

LEVITICUS 23:40

Meditation

An evergreen shade-giving plant that thrives where there is little water seems a miraculous gift from God to desert-dwelling peoples. Thus the palms of the Holy Land were highly valued in the time of Christ and were the consummate symbol of life. Our Palm Sunday Mass is based on these plants, and it has become the most beautiful and bittersweet celebration of the Christian year. We prepare to leave the darkness of winter and Lent behind for the life of the coming spring. We yearn to witness the eternal light of the Resurrection, but Christ's impending suffering and death add an undercurrent of sadness to the ritual blessing of living palms. The fronds, once blessed, are a sacramental to bring home to adorn our own household shrines. They can be given to another person as a sign of reconciliation. In northern regions where it is too cold for palms, people use willow rods or attach paper flowers and ribbons to the top of a stick or staff. If some palm is available, a tiny sliver of it is attached to these colorful bouquets.

The weary traveler and his equally fatigued camel felt their spirits rise and new vigor strengthen them when the waving palm tops of a distant oasis were sighted; water, food, shade, and perhaps company, lay ahead. It was natural that palm branches should become the emblem of welcome, public homage, and journey's end.

Alastair I. Mackay, *Farming and Gardening in the Bible*, 1950

PLANT

Date Palm

Phoenix dactylifera

The Holy Land we know today bears little resemblance to its former glory. In historic texts, we learn that the region was once filled with date-palm groves, and first-century historian Josephus describes a grove seven miles long near Jericho. Palmyra was named for its palms, and Bethany, derived from the Hebrew *bet teainah,* means "house of dates." The date palm, *Phoenix dactylifera,* became the symbol of life because it provided the people with food, oil, and shelter in the desert. In addition, the presence of palms at Middle Eastern oases made them a sign of shade and water that could be recognized at great distances.

Date palms are dioecious plants, which means that a male palm and a female palm must coexist in order to produce fruit. One of the ways that ancient conquerors punished the vanquished was to cut down their male palms so that female trees failed to produce fruit for a very long time. Only after new male palms were planted and had matured enough to produce pollen did the date crop reappear. For desert peoples, loss of this valuable food source spelled certain disaster.

The padres of the early California missions carried dried dates as food, and they planted date palms in California from the leftover pits. Although these palms did not produce fruit, they did provide valuable thatching material and, most of all, served in their Holy Week ceremonies and decorations. Some of these palms survived into the twentieth century, long after the missions were abandoned, attesting to their longevity. Today the only fruit-producing date palms in North America are grown in the inland deserts of southern California and Arizona.

In the contemporary landscape, the closely related Canary Island date palm, *Phoenix canariensis,* proves a nearly identical substitute with far better cold hardiness. These palms are more attractive, with larger, more filled-out fronds that can reach fifteen feet in length.

You may be surprised to discover that there are some palms that will take a hard frost and survive. The Mediterranean fan palm *Chamerops humilis* is a slow-growing, many-trunked landscape palm reputed to survive down to 0°F, but only mature specimens can be reliable to this extreme. It is safer to consider this fan palm hardy to no lower than 6°F. Small stature and a clumping habit produce a picturesque palm that grows to no more than ten feet tall, making a great landscape specimen. If you live in a marginal climate and long for the tropics, and if your church wishes to grow its own palm fronds for Holy Week, *Chamerops humilis* is an ideal candidate that is widely available.

Canary Island Date Palm

Phoenix canariensis

Zone 9

Type: Evergreen palm

Origin: Canary Islands

Habitat: Full sun

Size: 30 feet tall and as wide

Plant: Anytime, from containers

Notable feature: More beautiful and hardy than the date palm

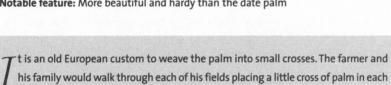

*I*t is an old European custom to weave the palm into small crosses. The farmer and his family would walk through each of his fields placing a little cross of palm in each one. We may sanctify our own garden to Christ in the very same way.

Good Friday

Jesus went out with his disciples across the Kidron valley to where there was a garden, into which he and his disciples entered.

JOHN 18:1

Weaving a crown out of thorns, they placed it on his head, and a reed in his right hand. And kneeling before him, they mocked him, saying, "Hail, King of the Jews!"

MATTHEW 27:29

We are witnesses of all that he did both in the country of the Jews and [in] Jerusalem. They put him to death by hanging him on a tree.

ACTS OF THE APOSTLES 10:39

There was a vessel filled with common wine. So they put a sponge soaked in wine on a sprig of hyssop and put it up to his mouth.

JOHN 19:29

Now in the place where he had been crucified there was a garden, and in the garden a new tomb, in which no one had yet been buried.

JOHN 19:41

After he had taken the body down, he wrapped it in a linen cloth and laid him in a rock-hewn tomb in which no one had yet been buried.

LUKE 23:53

Meditation

There may be more references to plants in the passion and death of Christ than in any other event in the Bible. The entire story can be told through its plants. Jesus was betrayed by Judas in the Garden of Gethsemane, which was actually an orchard of olive trees. The Romans made Jesus hold a reed as they mocked him. He wore a painful crown of thorny twigs. He was crucified on a tree, and in his last moments of life was offered a wine-soaked sprig of hyssop to wet his tongue. He was buried in a garden tomb, and even the burial shroud itself was made of cloth woven from fibers of the flax plant.

On this sad momentous day we find great inspiration in the garden. Others did, too, for throughout Christian history many legends have appeared surrounding the wood of the true cross. The stories explain that the willow perpetually weeps and the aspen quakes from their reluctant roles as wood of the cross. However, it is likely the true cross was made of olive wood or cedar, the only two large trees of the Holy Land.

Passionflower

Passiflora spp.

The passionflower vine is another plant we can trace back to early Catholic missions. It was first collected in South America in 1610 by a Mexican Augustinian friar, Emanuel De Villegas. He was captivated by the exotic flowers and had drawings made of the beautiful and intricately detailed blossom.

These he sent back to Rome, where Jesuit Jacomo Bosio connected the flower itself to the passion of Christ. Each part of the flower represents a different element of the Passion. The padres who established the California missions grew the flower and used it to teach the botanically minded Native Americans the story of Christ's death.

Passionflower
Passiflora caerulea

Zone 8

Type: Evergreen vine

Origin: Brazil

Habitat: Sun or part shade where protected

Size: Spreading to 20 feet

Plant: Anytime, from containers

Notable feature: Edible fruit

The Judas Tree

Only one Scripture passage points to the plant commonly known as the Judas tree, *Cercis siliquastrum*. It is a close relative of our own American redbuds. Matthew's Gospel states that Judas hanged himself on the redbud tree and from that day forward it bloomed purple, the color of the Lenten vestments.

*I*n Europe, farmers and gardeners believe that anything planted on Good Friday will grow vigorously because the earth is sanctified by drops of Christ's blood and by his burial.

The Shroud of Turin

Just when it seemed as though everyone accepted the Shroud of Turin as the ingenious fakery of a medieval artist, botanists found interesting evidence to support the shroud's authenticity. Carbon dating done in the late 1980s indicated that the shroud had a medieval origin. Some microbiologists believe the carbon-dating process responded to the plant fungus and bacteria buildup on the linen cloth, not to the older fibers underneath. In the late 1990s, botanists reexamined pollen samples that had been taken from the shroud in the early 1970s. Among other things, they found embedded in the cloth the pollen of *Zygophyllum dumosum*, a bean caper that grows only in the Holy Land. It is even more specific to a small range between Jericho and Jerusalem, proving that the fibers had been spun and woven in Israel. The discovery of the pollen and the identification of its DNA supercede the irregularities of carbon dating. It is likely we do have the burial cloth of Christ, complete with its microscopic evidence of that first Good Friday over two thousand years ago.

Easter

And they said to her, "Woman, why are you weeping?" She said to them, "They have taken my Lord, and I don't know where they laid him." When she had said this, she turned around and saw Jesus there, but did not know it was Jesus. Jesus said to her, "Woman, why are you weeping? Whom are you looking for?" She thought it was the gardener and said to him, "Sir, if you carried him away, tell me where you laid him, and I will take him." Jesus said to her, "Mary!" She turned and said to him in Hebrew, "Rabbouni," which means Teacher.

JOHN 20:13–16

Meditation

It is moving to think that the risen Christ was so like a gardener that Mary didn't recognize him at first. This event sanctifies gardening, for this calling was important enough for John to include it in his Gospel. Perhaps becoming a gardener satisfies us so deeply because it is a quasireligious act. Unlike other hobbies that are strictly in the realm of man, the cultivation of living plants becomes much more than mere science or aesthetics. It was no mistake that the early church fathers placed the Resurrection so close to the spring equinox, the time of sowing, when all plant life returns to green the countryside. Spring is also the greening of the gardener's soul, for it is the coming forth of our whole passionate world of plants after the cold, dark, and seemingly endless winter.

When winter binds the earth with ice, all the glory of the field perishes with its flowers.
But in the spring-time when the Lord overcame Hell, bright grass shoots up
and buds come forth. . . . Gather these first-fruits and . . . bear them to the churches and
wreath the altars.

Bishop of Poitiers

PLANT

Tansy

Tanacetum vulgare

This old-fashioned herb has long been associated with Lent and Easter for both religious and practical reasons. Tansy pudding or tansy cakes were made in honor of the bitter herbs eaten with the Passover meal and as a symbol of Christ's suffering. Tansy was eaten as a medicinal in early spring to expel intestinal parasites that often resulted from a poor winter diet. The Puritans brought tansy with them to the New World because the dried leaves repelled household insect pests. Its lovely yellow flowers dry much like yarrow, and tansy's resiliency has caused it to naturalize all across America.

Omnia vere vigent et veris
tempore florent
Et totus fervet Veneris
dulcedine mundus.
Spring clothes the fields and decks
the flower grove,
And all creation glows with life
and love.

MEDIEVAL TANSY PUDDING

Recipe adapted from John Nott, *The Cook's and Confectioner's Dictionary,* 1726

> ½ pint milk
> 1 Tbsp. butter
> 3 oz. fresh white bread crumbs
> 2 Tbsp. honey
> 2 tsp. finely chopped tansy leaves
> 2 eggs, beaten

Preheat oven to 350°F. Boil the milk and butter together and pour over the bread crumbs. Set aside for 30 minutes. Add the sugar or honey and the tansy leaves to the eggs; then mix with the bread crumbs and bake the mixture in a glass loaf pan until set. Serve cold with honey and cream.

Tansy

Tanacetum vulgare

Zone 4

Type: Perennial flower

Origin: Europe

Habitat: Full sun

Size: 4 to 5 feet tall and 3 to 4 feet wide

Plant: Spring, from containers

Notable feature: Aromatic herb

*I*n Great Britain there is an ancient tradition of watching the sun rise on Easter morning, which is the source of the popularity of Easter sunrise services. But in the old days, the Celtic druids believed that the sun danced with joy. Many people have reported seeing different colors as the sun rises on the morning of the Resurrection.

A voice says, "Cry out!"
　　　I answer, "What shall I cry out?"
"All mankind is grass,
　　　and all their glory like the flower of the field.
The grass withers, the flower wilts,
　　　when the breath of the Lord blows upon it.
　　　[So then, the people is the grass.]
Though the grass withers and the flower wilts,
the word of our God stands forever."

Isaiah 40:6–8

April

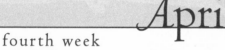

fourth week

Meditation

There is nothing more humble on earth than the wild grasses that live for just a short time after spring rains revive the hillsides. The grasses do not demand much, and yet they work diligently, filling their important role in nature. Grasses keep the earth from blowing away or washing into the rivers. They feed the animals that come to graze, and they offer seeds to the birds. Wild grasses are like the people of the world who do not achieve fame or create great works. They are the millions who labor day after day in the humble acts of living well, honest and true. A grass fulfills its destiny by growing rich and green and scattering its seed to the wind to beget more grasses.

Lying in the sunshine among the buttercups and dandelions of May, scarcely higher in intelligence than the minute tenants of that mimic wilderness, our earliest recollections are of grass; and when the fitful fever is ended, and the foolish wrangle of the market and forum is closed, grass heals over the scar which our descent into the bosom of the earth has made, and the carpet of the infant becomes the blanket of the dead.

Senator John James Ingalls, *In Praise of Bluegrass,* **1872**

Gardening

As the weather warms, your dormant lawn will come back to life. The dead stems will begin to green as thousands of tiny leaf blades rise up out of the chaff. Some parts of the lawn will not green up, though, and these will need attention if they are to heal and grow properly. One of the biggest threats to healthy turf grass is soil that has been compacted so tightly that roots cannot penetrate to any depth. The shallow roots fail to find water or nourishment, and no matter how often you reseed these barren places, grass will refuse to grow. You must remedy this compacted earth by puncturing the hard ground with a spading fork or aerating machine as deeply as you can. Then fill the holes with composted steer manure, and the resident earthworms will do the rest. Reseed only after you have aerated the soil, opening the way for deep rooting in the future.

PLANT

Maiden Grass

Miscanthus sinensis 'Gracillimus'

Until recent years, grasses were thought to belong only in turf, and all other grasses were weeds. Yet in the wild, we admire the tall prairie grass when its seed heads are riffled by the wind, and we think them animated and beautiful. Gardeners are discovering that these giant grasses are incredibly beautiful textural plants with bold architectural forms. The maiden grasses under *Miscanthus sinensis* cultivars are very cold hardy, require little care, and are fabulous in every season. In spring, bright green fountains of grass flower in tall, wind-pollinated spikes.

The special clumsy beauty of this particular cold on this April day in this field under these clouds is a holiness consecrated to God by His own Art, and it declares the glory of God.

Thomas Merton,
Seeds of Contemplation, **1949**

These mature into fluffy seed heads before the plant goes dormant in the fall, taking on outstanding colors of gold and russet. Do not cut these grasses back until early spring so that in the dead of winter their skeletons stand in dramatic silhouette against snow. They remain beautiful in icy cold winds while all else has retreated into the earth to sleep.

Maiden Grass

Miscanthus sinensis 'Gracillimus'

Zone 5

Type: Ornamental grass

Origin: Asia

Habitat: Full sun

Size: 6 to 8 feet tall and 3 to 5 feet wide

Plant: Spring or fall, from containers

Each blade of grass has its spot on earth whence it draws its life, its strength; and so is man rooted to the land from which he draws his faith together with his life.

Joseph Conrad, *Lord Jim*

Lord, remind me that millions of people are too often taken for granted. I must remember that each soul is created and loved by you, much as you give life to each blade of grass. There is a purpose for every living thing no matter how small, weak, or humble it may appear. Amen.

In Britain, very old stone churches were cold in winter, lacked kneelers, and featured a Latin Mass far longer than today's service. From the time of the Norman Conquest to the late nineteenth century, farmers would dig up a big hassock of tufted grass from the pasture and bring it into the church to use as a soft "bull front kneeler."

May

Madonna Lily

Lilium candidum

Zone 5

Type: Summer bulb

Origin: Asia Minor

Habitat: Full sun and well-drained soil

Size: 3 to 4 feet tall and 1 foot wide

Plant: Fall or very early spring, from dormant bulbs

Notable feature: Fragrant flowers; easy to grow in suitable climates

Madonna Lily

Lilium candidum

The lily is a well-known symbol of Christian purity and of resurrection, which is why it figures so largely into our Easter celebrations. In cultivation since early biblical times, it became linked to virginity, both that of Mary and of the early virgin martyrs. In paintings of the Annunciation, a lily is often positioned between Mary and the archangel Gabriel. In Europe the species blooms around the Feast of the Visitation.

I rejoice heartily in the Lord,
  in my God is the joy of my soul;
For he has clothed me with a robe of salvation,
  and wrapped me in a mantle of justice,
Like a bridegroom adorned with a diadem,
  like a bride bedecked with her jewels.
As the earth brings forth its plants,
  and a garden makes its growth spring up,
So will the Lord God make justice and praise
  spring up before all the nations.

ISAIAH 61:10–11

May

Meditation

This week marks the beginning of the most beautiful and fertile months of the year. The spring lambs are born, flowers bloom, and the whole world is green with new plants. The ancient agrarian rites recognize this as a time of growth and increase, of procreation and love. It was dedicated to the Roman goddesses Maia and Flora, both honored throughout the empire by great floral celebrations. In Christian times these same festivities were given over to Mary, with bouquets and flower garlands used liberally in her honor. For those who garden, it is a busy time of planting and caring for young plants during fickle weather. But each act in the garden is one of celebration.

Gardening

Although we call it planting, much of what we do this time of year is really transplanting. Whether it is moving a plant from one part of the garden to the other or burying a formerly potted plant in garden soil, relocation is always traumatic for the plant. Roots are sensitive and quickly dry out when exposed to air. Your goal should be to reduce the trauma as much as possible through proper timing and careful handling.

Always gather all your plants, tools, and supplies before you start planting so that the poor plants won't languish while you break away to hunt down a lost tool. Transplanting should be done in cool, overcast conditions, ideally just before a rain shower. In the real world, we are forced to plant when we have time, but you should avoid midday. Water the plant deeply right after you put it in the ground, particularly if the soil is dry, to collapse any trapped air pockets in the root zone. Then keep a sharp eye out for the first signs of wilt on hot days.

PLANT

Pot Marigold
Calendula officinalis

This marvelous European annual bedding flower is so eager to bloom that it was named *Calendula* as it was thought to flower the whole "calendar" year. In reality, in the West and South, *Calendula* is more likely to bloom in late winter, and due to its widespread use in garlands for the Feast of the Annunciation in March, it became the flower of our Blessed Mother. Do not confuse this ancient Old World genus with New World marigolds of genus *Tagetes*. Plants are available in a taller cutting-flower form for the back of a border or as dwarf bedding plants for edges, massing, and pots. Its cheerful daisy flowers have long been used as wound coagulants and were grown for battlefield use as recently as the First World War. The edible petals from either the yellow or orange types, once used to color cheddar cheese, are vibrant additions to salads or garnishes along with *Viola tricolor,* commonly known as Johnny-jump-up.

Pot Marigold

Calendula officinalis

All zones

Type: Cool-season annual

Origin: Europe

Habitat: Full sun

Size: Varies 12 to 24 inches tall and as wide

Plant: Fall or spring in cooler climates, winter in warm ones

Notable feature: Orange or yellow edible flower petals for salad or garnish

Mary, you were the fertile ground in which the Holy Spirit sowed the seed of Redemption two thousand years ago. Let your spirit reside within my garden this year so that I might nurture these living plants and flowers as a gift to you. Amen.

For see, the winter is past, the rains are over and gone.

The flowers appear on the earth, the time of pruning the vines has come,

and the song of the dove is heard in our land.

The fig tree puts forth its figs, and the vines, in bloom, give forth fragrance.

Arise, my beloved, my beautiful one, and come!

SONG OF SONGS 2:11–13

Meditation

By this week in May there is little doubt that winter has passed. The warming days evoke a primal response in us to go out amid the plants and flowers and tend them. Often we are seized with the desire to walk out into the countryside to see the vivid greens of new leaves and the dainty wildflowers that rise in the meadows. For gardeners it is a strong compulsion that cannot be denied, and any depression lingering after winter is quickly dispelled in the sunshine. Now is the time to get out of the house and at least sit on a porch or patio in the sun. The longer days and more intense sunlight signal the body and the spirit, reminding us that no matter how long, dark, and dreary the journey through winter may have been, the journey is over—we have reached this glorious spring.

Gardening

In this part of spring, we are just gearing up while the plants are in a rapid state of change. A perennial requires tremendous energy to regrow its stems and leaves, not to mention develop its blooms. Trees must produce an entire canopy of new leaves over the span of just a few weeks. We should spend a great deal of time in our garden observing, ready to offer fertilizer to plants that seem too yellow or sluggish. Use manure if you are an organic gardener, spreading it around each plant, cultivating lightly to incorporate it into the soil. Long-lasting, all-purpose commercial fertilizer granules spread and raked in will gradually dissolve with the rain to fortify the plant with its major food-group needs. It's a good idea to keep a bag of inexpensive generic 16-16-16 granules on hand to toss around your shrubs and trees. In this season it is vital to inspect plants daily for changes and subtle indications of need. It makes little difference if you are in the garden to work or just inspect while relishing the morning sun and a steaming cup of coffee.

PLANT

Japanese Camellia

Camellia japonica

The camellia is among the most beautiful of all evergreen shrubs and thrives in the dappled shade of the forest floor, much like the rhododendron. In the forest, soil nutrients are concentrated on the surface of the soil just underneath a layer of decomposing leaf litter. Camellias evolved with very shallow fibrous roots that feed off this layer and spread out over a large area. For this reason you should dig a hole for a new camellia far wider than the hole is deep, and you must never cultivate the soil around its base where the tender feeder roots are most prevalent. Instead, mulch the plants to keep the soil evenly moist and the roots adequately protected during hot summers. This plant has more than one hundred varieties, with flowers ranging from single to fully double in many shades from white to carmine red. Buy small plants and avoid planting them on a western exposure, to protect them from the hot afternoon sun.

Japanese Camellia

Camellia japonica

Zone 8

Type: Evergreen flowering shrub

Origin: Asia

Habitat: Morning sun or filtered shade

Size: To 20 feet tall with age

Plant: Spring or fall, from containers

Lord, remind me often to go out into my garden and spend peaceful time there. I get so busy, but I know that it is during these precious times that I am closest to you. As I grow intimate with every plant in my garden, let me become more sensitive to them in this small sanctuary. Amen.

Our garden camellia is closely related to the *Camellia sinensis*, the source plant of English tea. This tea was first discovered by Shennong, emperor of China in 2737 BC, where it was used as a medicinal beverage. By the eleventh century, Buddhist monks drank it to keep awake during their long religious ceremonies.

KAMEL'S *CAMELLIA JAPONICA*

Camellia is a genus of flowering shrubs native to a large part of China and Japan, where they became popular garden plants. Eventually, they spread throughout the South Pacific. It was in the Philippines that an Austrian Jesuit missionary trained in the botanical and medical sciences became the first Westerner to take note of camellia. Georg Josef Kamel, S.J. (1661–1704) was stationed in what is now the Philippines, where he founded a large apothecary garden at the Jesuit College in Manila. Kamel studied all the wild and garden plants of Luzon Island, then sent his journals, drawings, and collected specimens to leading European botanists. Recipients of his work included Carolus Linnaeus, the father of the binomial nomenclature system used to classify all living things. Among these shipments were the seeds of the celebrated *Camellia japonica,* and Linnaeus honored their discoverer by naming the genus in the latinized form of Kamel's name. It is interesting to note that Kamel is likely the first to have sent seed of another plant to Europe, that of a woody climbing shrub truly native to the Philippine jungles. Linnaeus later named it *Strychnos ignatii,* or Jesuit's bean, for St. Ignatius and his missionary priests. From the large seeds of this plant, French chemists first isolated strychnine in 1818 and produced many valuable medicines. The bean was also believed to be an effective treatment for cholera.

Be patient, therefore, brothers, until the coming of the Lord. See how the farmer waits for the precious fruit of the earth, being patient with it until it receives the early and the late rains. You too must be patient. Make your hearts firm, because the coming of the Lord is at hand.

JAMES 5:7–8

*M*ay

MAY 15 FEAST OF ST. ISIDORE THE FARMER

Meditation

St. Isidore the farmer, a humble tenth-century Spanish peasant, spent long days in the field behind his plow. It was said that when he grew too weary, angels took over the plow to allow him rest and time to pray. The first Spanish colonial farmers of the New World brought with them their patron saint of field labor and agriculture. In the uncertain conditions of the arid Southwest, St. Isidore was often invoked in times of drought. Each spring at planting time the people carried their carved statue of San Isidro in procession through the fields to bless the crops and ensure a good harvest. Today he is particularly beloved by the migrant farmworkers who labor long days in American fields, orchards, and vineyards.

> *He [the farmer] is the agent or the representative of society to guard and to subdue the surface of the earth; and he is the agent of the divinity that made it. He must exercise his dominion with due regard to all these obligations. He is a trustee. The productiveness of the earth must increase from generation to generation: this is also his obligation. He must handle all his materials, remembering man and remembering God. A man cannot be a good farmer unless he is a religious man.*
>
> **Liberty Hyde Bailey, *The Holy Earth*, 1918**

Gardening

Ralph Waldo Emerson said, "What is a weed? A plant whose virtues have not yet been discovered." These plants in which we find little virtue are abundant in the spring garden as every wintering seed sprouts to life. So too do the rootlets that have lain dormant, waiting to grow in the moist temperatures and soft earth of this season. Now is the time to do away with these less virtuous plants before they flourish into recalcitrant adulthood.

The best weed-pulling is done during or just after a light rain, when the earth is so soft the roots find little purchase against a gentle tug. Strive to take out the entire taproot of a dandelion or dock it so that it will not grow back. Dig out the whole clump of nut sedge or Bermuda grass, and do not let it compost or it may further infect the garden. Take these perennial *plantas non gratas* straight to the garbage can. The work you do now in removing these long-lived invasive weeds will pay off a hundredfold later in the year.

PLANT

Roman Chamomile

Anthemis nobilis

This virtuous plant is an old Mediterranean native that sprang up behind the expanding Roman armies. The Romans valued chamomile as a medicinal and grew it with garlic at all of their outposts. From these gardens it spread all over Britain and then to the American colonies, where tea of the flowers was a household remedy for upset stomach. Although these sweet white daisies and aromatic foliage are lovely in the garden, chamomile remains a weed to the farmer who must contend with its exuberance amid his row crops. Chamomile's earth-hugging habit makes it a lovely ground cover, and it will reseed itself liberally once introduced into a garden. When you buy chamomile in small pots at the garden center, be sure it is the perennial *Anthemis nobilis,* which will come back each year on the same roots. The nearly identical relative, English chamomile, *Matricaria chamomilla,* is an annual best planted from seed but is an equally valued medicinal.

Roman Chamomile

Anthemis nobilis

Zone 3

Type: Perennial herb

Origin: Southern Europe

Habitat: Full sun or part shade

Size: 1 foot tall, spreading to 2 feet wide

Plant: Spring, from seed or containers

Notable feature: Herbal tea remedies upset stomach

Lord, every living thing is imbued with virtue because you have created it. As I pull these spring weeds, keep me mindful that these plants may have once contributed to the diet and health of people in the past. Help me to learn their names, their place of origin, and their ancient uses so that they are no longer just weeds but virtuous plants that are merely out of place. Amen.

When he was in Bethany reclining at table in the house of Simon the leper, a woman came with an alabaster jar of perfumed oil, costly genuine spikenard. She broke the alabaster jar and poured it on his head. There were some who were indignant. "Why has there been this waste of perfumed oil?"

MARK 14:3–4

Mary took a liter of costly perfumed oil made from genuine aromatic nard and anointed the feet of Jesus and dried them with her hair; the house was filled with the fragrance of the oil.

JOHN 12:3

May

Meditation

From plants come great sensual experiences. The biblical nard, or spikenard, used to anoint Christ is derived from the root of a plant native to Asia Minor called *Nardostachys jatamansi,* which is related to our garden valerians. Throughout history, fresh cut flowers and the perfumes made from them were as precious as gold, because they masked the unattractive smells of human habitation. Many of the plants we grow today are among the most fragrant of all, and one can imagine that had the lilac been known in Jerusalem, the women would have anointed Jesus with its oil. When we grow such rich fragrance our world becomes anointed with God's very own perfumes in their pure and natural state.

If odors, or if taste may work satisfaction, they are both so sovereign in plants, and so comfortable, that no confection of the Apothecaries can equal their excellent virtue. But these delights are in the outward senses: the principal delight is in the mind, singularly enriched with the knowledge of these visible things, setting forth to us the invisible workmanship of Almighty God.

John Gerard, preface to *The Herball,* 1597

May Fourth Week   85

Gardening

This month the lilacs bloom across the northern states, heralding the coming of summer. These large shrubs should be cared for after bloom to encourage large full flowers for next year. All of the soft suckering growth that comes from the base of the plant should be pulled up by hand. Dig around the base of the sucker to find the point at which it originates and sever there. Do not sever the sucker at the surface of the soil; doing so may actually encourage the sucker to become more established in the next growing season. After you have done this, loosen the top few inches of soil in a radius around the plant from its trunk to the tips of the branches. Spread a layer of composted steer manure up to two inches deep over the newly turned earth. This will feed the roots and keep them cool through the heat of summer.

PLANT

Common Lilac

Syringa vulgaris

Our common lilac is so plentiful it seems a native to America or at least to western Europe, but it has only naturalized here. The lilac is actually from Turkey and has been grown in Europe since the sixteenth century. The French are credited with the development of modern lilac culture through a host of new species collected by nineteenth-century Catholic missionaries in China.

This vigorous shrub is easy to grow and withstands cold, making it one of the best deciduous shrubs for northern climates. Lilacs can be disappointing in southern regions where plants decline for lack of a sufficient winter chill. A mature lilac will reach immense proportions over time; consequently, they are popular screen-hedge material. When cut and brought indoors, the lilac's large, potently scented flowers will perfume an entire room. Modern hybrids offer lilacs of shorter stature for small gardens, lilacs that will thrive in slightly warmer climates, and varieties with flower color from snow white through pink to the traditional purple.

Common Lilac

Syringa vulgaris

Zone 4

Type: Deciduous flowering shrub

Origin: Eurasia

Habitat: Full sun

Size: Variable; 8 to 10 feet tall and about 6 feet wide

Plant: Spring or fall, from containers

Notable feature: Highly fragrant early spring flowers

Lord, you have created scented flowers to add fragrance to our lives. Remind me each time I linger, enjoying the perfume of lilac or gardenia or jasmine, that you are the fragrance of my spiritual life. Unless I stop to smell the flowers, I will miss out on the enjoyment of my garden and your quiet presence in my life. Amen.

*I*t was once considered bad luck to bring cut lilacs indoors, but this is only the legacy of lilacs as a cloaking fragrance for the smell of death. The odor was a serious problem, especially during summertime, because deceased family members were usually laid out in the parlor for a time so that all could visit and pay their respects.

BROTHER STEFAN'S GARDEN

We do not think of Poland as a center for ornamental plant breeding, nor do we connect a religious vocation with hybridization of the most beautiful flowers in the world. Yet the work of one humble monk has come to the attention of the global horticultural community because of his extraordinary plant creations.

Eighty-five-year-old Brother Stefan Franczak carries on the tradition of plant sciences that other Jesuit botanists began centuries ago. He was born in 1917 on a farm in central Poland, was educated at an agricultural college, and graduated in 1946, after the end of World War II. In 1948, he joined the Society of Jesus as a brother at the Jesuit college on Rakowiecka Street, where he was put in charge of its vegetable and fruit garden. The garden had been badly damaged during the war, and the Jesuits had planned to build a new church on that site. They were restrained by a government that preferred that they use the space to create a public garden. Brother Stefan was charged with transforming the site from a fruit and vegetable garden into a beautiful public space.

Despite difficult circumstances under an oppressive Communist government, Brother Stefan managed to use his connections with other monastic communities to obtain plants, catalogs, and literature on various plant species from around the world. His greatest interests lay in three genera: clematis vines, daylilies, and bearded iris. Faced with the task of beautifying old stone fences and tree stumps on the site, he decided that clematis vines were the ideal plant with which to cover these things up. Brother Stefan managed to collect a large number of clematis from all over Poland, along with many from France, Britain,

and the United States. He began growing quantities of the plants to sell in order to raise money to buy more new plants. Eventually he turned to breeding and engineered crosses between the Polish plants and the imported hybrids.

Brother Stefan's methods were quite like those of another monk, Gregor Mendel, both of whom grew large numbers of seedlings and systematically selected those with new or superior qualities. Brother Stefan's primary goal was to find larger flowers with new colors and more dramatic stamens that contrasted with the sepals. Seedlings with potential were planted around the garden in different exposures to gauge their vigor and adaptability. Brother Stefan observed many of his plants in the garden for ten years or more before he deemed them a suitable variety.

Although Brother Stefan had been breeding new plants for decades, the Communist regime made it difficult for him to introduce them to the rest of Europe. In 1980, with the collapse of the old government, he was free to spread his accumulation of new plants throughout the world. In 1982, Brother Stefan's first clematis—a variety he named to honor the Holy Father, 'Jan Pawel II'—was presented at the Chelsea Flower Show in London.

Brother Stefan names all his clematis after famous people of Poland. Perhaps his most famous clematis is 'Kardynal Wyszynski,' named for Cardinal Stefan Wyszynski, who was head of the Catholic Church in Poland for almost thirty years during a particularly brutal stretch of Communist government.

Brother Stefan's clematis have received numerous gold medals in Holland and the Award of Garden Merit in England. His plants are widely available in the United States and are distributed in Europe via the nursery of Szczepan Marczyński, near Warsaw.

Brother Stefan continues to work long days in his garden. He belongs to many international horticultural organizations that have helped to bring his outstanding new contributions to our attention. But most of all, Brother Stefan points out that the natural connection between the spiritual life and that of the garden is a most rewarding path to God.

See pictures of all of Brother Stefan's clematis at the Szczepan Marczyński Nursery Web site: http://www.clematis.com.pl.

June

Strawberry

Fragaria hybrid

Zone 2 (variable)

Type: Fruiting perennial

Origin: South America

Habitat: Full sun

Size: 6 inches tall and 12 inches wide

Plant: Spring or fall, from containers

Notable feature: Edible berries

Strawberry

Fragaria hybrid

The strawberry plant has become a symbol of Mary's sweetness and purity, but each of its individual parts is connected to different aspects of Christianity. The bright red fruit represents the blood shed by Christ and the martyrs. Like St. Patrick's shamrock, its three-part leaf is a sign of the Holy Trinity. The five petals of each blossom are the five wounds of Jesus. It was once a popular custom to plant strawberries and violets together in the garden to suggest humility. Strawberries remain quite popular in the home garden and may be divided every two or three years to increase fruit production.

I am a flower of Sharon,
      a lily of the valley.
As a lily among thorns,
      so is my beloved among women.
As an apple tree among the trees of the woods,
      so is my lover among men.
I delight to rest in his shadow,
      and his fruit is sweet to my mouth....
Strengthen me with raisin cakes,
      refresh me with apples,
      for I am faint with love.

SONG OF SONGS 2:1–5

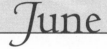

June

first week

Meditation

This month is a traditional time for weddings. The coming together of man and woman is one of the most beautiful and important sacraments. This pairing of the sexes is reflected in all living things, be they birds or flowers. It is celebrated with white to underscore the purity of lifelong union. The color white also represents virginity, which currently seems unimportant to many but is the cornerstone of human survival. Just as a grower keeps his greenhouse scrupulously clean to ensure that young seedlings are healthy and disease free, virginity is the ancient means of ensuring that a marriage flourishes, a family line continues, and the clan or tribe will never die out.

If the Father deigns to touch with divine power the cold and pulseless heart of the buried acorn and to make it burst forth from its prison walls, will He leave neglected in the earth the soul of man made in the image of his Creator?

William Jennings Bryan, *The Prince of Peace*

Gardening

Love is to marriage just as water is to a plant facing the first wave of hot summer weather. When mentally stressed, we may reach into the well of love for strength. Our garden plants may draw moisture from deep underground when temperatures soar. Those plants in pots and containers, however, are more vulnerable and require a bit more attention.

Potted plants sometimes fail to thrive because of a dry pocket in the soil. When the plant is watered, the water simply flows through a few channels of least resistance and bypasses the still-dry pocket. To ensure that your root ball is thoroughly wet, begin with a large bucket, add some water to the bottom and place the potted plant inside. Water the plant until the level of water draining out of the plant into the bucket is about halfway up the side of the plant's pot. This water creates a pressure equilibrium that forces water to remain in the root ball to saturate it completely. Let the pot sit for an hour or more, then remove the pot and give it a half-strength application of liquid fertilizer. Soon after you will see a transformation and growth spurt.

Bridal Wreath

Spiraea prunifolia

This beloved and old-fashioned, deciduous flowering shrub blooms in long arches of small, snow-white flowers. Its color and early June blooming season led to its traditional use in headpieces worn by country brides in America. Bridal wreath is hardy to zone 3 and is reliable everywhere but in the warmest regions. Introduced to the West in 1845, this Japanese native has a number of improved cultivars. It will naturalize almost anywhere and can be a good foundation shrub that is incredible when moonlight reflects off its snow-white flowers. It is valued by flower arrangers and landscape gardeners alike.

Bridal Wreath

Spiraea prunifolia

Zone 3

Type: Deciduous flowering shrub

Origin: Asia

Habitat: Full sun

Size: 6 feet tall and as wide

Plant: Spring or fall, from containers

Notable feature: Long white sprays woven into bride's wreath

My spirit has become dry because it forgets to feed on you.

St. John of the Cross

Lord, remind me to be as yielding as water in my relationships with loved ones. Grant me the patience of water, and like it, use love to gradually move mountains and soften hearts with time.

Notice how the flowers grow. They do not toil or spin. But I tell you, not even Solomon in all his splendor was dressed like one of them. If God so clothes the grass in the field that grows today and is thrown into the oven tomorrow, will he not much more provide for you, O you of little faith? As for you, do not seek what you are to eat and what you are to drink, and do not worry anymore. All the nations of the world seek for these things, and your Father knows that you need them. Instead, seek his kingdom, and these other things will be given you besides.

LUKE 12:27–31

June

second week

Meditation

All agricultural peoples live an uncertain daily existence that is as subject to disaster today as it was millennia ago. Our daily anxieties are nothing in the larger scheme of things, and yet we worry whether we can buy a better car or bigger house or go on a more exotic vacation. When we place our hopes in such material things we are destined for disappointment. We should be fretting over our lack of prayer time, missed Sunday Masses, and estrangement from our moral values. Real disasters, whether natural or man-made, cause our worries about car or vacation to vanish in an instant, proving how unimportant they really are. Our goal should be to return to God and the simple peace of the garden when we feel stressed or worried, rather than try to ease these anxieties with the false hopes of a material world.

Gardening

June is the month when our roses produce their first great flourish of blooms. A rose should not be treated tenderly, but rigorously pruned throughout the growing season to stimulate more blooms. Novice gardeners clip close to the spent flower, leaving behind the long gangly stem that will only produce smaller, weaker secondary blooms. The proper method is to cut the flower off at the root of its stem, where the rose will produce a second stem of nearly the same size and strength. This aggressive pruning will ensure a very large new bloom and robust growth all season. A good rule of thumb is to trace the stem back to a point where it is no smaller than the diameter of a pencil, and then cut just above the nearest outward-facing bud. Fertilize heavily and your roses will bloom without pause all season long.

The "Indestructible" Hedge Rose
Rosa rugosa

If you have avoided roses because your climate is too cold or you simply don't have the time to battle diseases, do not despair. This rose, sold as species *Rosa rugosa,* is among the hardiest roses on earth, surviving brutal winters to zone 3. It is virtually disease free and tolerant of both wind and salt spray. The plants develop into dense bushy shrubs that spread underground via traveling roots, which makes them ideal for use as hedges along driveways or fence lines. *Rugosas* bloom repeatedly, and some improved cultivars include yellow-flowering 'Topaz Jewel' and fragrant 'Buffalo Gal.' The fruit that develops if spent blossoms are not cut off is bright red and decorative in winter snow. In addition, the thick, vitamin-rich flesh of the rose hip makes it one of the herbalist's favorite medicines.

Rugosa Rose

Rosa rugosa

Zone 3

Type: Hardy rose

Origin: Asia

Habitat: Full sun

Size: 6 feet tall and as wide, spreading

Plant: Spring or fall, bare root or from containers

Notable feature: Large, fleshy hip is medicinal or decorative

Rose-Hip Tea for Colds

During the worst days of World War II, British imports of citrus fruits were cut off. Children began showing the first symptoms of scurvy, a debilitating disease caused by vitamin C deficiency. The search for a source sent everyone out into the countryside, and it was the fruit, or hip, of a briar rose that proved to contain more vitamin C ounce for ounce than oranges. Every rose hip in England was gathered and concentrated into a syrup that protected the children for the duration.

If you grow roses, such as rugosas, you will have a ready supply of this famous home remedy. Allow the rose fruit to mature, and then pick them as needed. To prepare a medicinal tea for flu and cold season you must peel the flesh away from the fibers and seeds inside. Wash the flesh and discard the fibers and seeds. Then crush three heaping tablespoons of fresh flesh and simmer in two cups of water for three to five minutes. Strain the tea and sweeten with liberal amounts of honey. Drink hot to discover its remarkably tart and fruity flavor.

Jesus, no matter how worried I become about the daily matters of life, help me to remember the lilies. Keep me mindful that if I trust in your Divine Mercy, you will never neglect my needs. And if my prayers are not immediately answered, do not allow me to succumb to despair. Let each new blooming rose be a sign that if I remain faithful all will be revealed in time. Amen.

For he gave me sound knowledge of existing things,
  that I might know the organization of the universe and the force of its elements,
The beginning and the end and the midpoint of times,
  the changes in the sun's course and the variations of the seasons.
Cycles of years, positions of the stars,
  natures of animals, tempers of beasts,
Powers of the winds and thoughts of men,
  uses of plants and virtues of roots—
Such things as are hidden I learned and such as are plain;
  for Wisdom, the artificer of all, taught me.

WISDOM 7:17–22

June

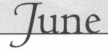

third week

Meditation

The desire to garden well is as strong for the experienced gardener as the novice because there is no end to what can be learned. However, this learning cannot be found in books but must come to a person after years of working with plants and with soil. In this, gardening is like self-knowledge and prayer, for we must speak frequently to God if he is to remain a familiar force in our lives.

Often our most important lessons come from mistakes made both in the garden and in life. Sometimes we suffer from the impact of our transgressions for years. Nothing takes the place of this experience, whether it is in cultivating our garden or turning the soil of the soul. And it is only through such practice and lessons learned that we will finally attain wisdom.

And a garden is a grand teacher. It teaches patience and careful watchfulness; it teaches industry and thrift; above all it teaches entire trust. "Paul planteth and Apollos watereth, but God giveth the increase." The good gardener knows with absolute certainty that if he does his part, if he gives the labour, the love, and every aid that his knowledge of his craft, experience of the conditions of his place, and exercise of his personal wit can work together to suggest, that so surely as he does this diligently and faithfully, so surely will God give the increase. Then with the honestly earned success comes the consciousness of encouragement to renewed effort, and, as it were, an echo of the gracious words, "Well done, good and faithful servant."

Gertrude Jekyll, ***Wood and Garden,*** **1899, reprinted 1983**

Gardening

As the days and, more important, the nights heat up, the population of insects that invade our garden explodes. The novice gardener views all bugs as bad when the wise gardener knows that some are highly beneficial. The praying mantis and the ladybug are important predators that you should protect at all costs.

In the past it was common practice to spray pesticides with the first crop of rose aphids, but these sprays destroyed the ladybugs and mantises that feed on aphids. Inevitably, due to large populations, a few aphids survived the pesticide to breed prolifically and infest the plant that was no longer protected by natural predators. Contemporary wisdom demands that gardeners learn to identify and make use of these beneficial insects. If aphids cloak your rose buds, simply buy a bag of live ladybugs at the garden center and put them to work for you. And it doesn't take a great deal of wisdom to realize that for every pest, God created a natural control that's a whole lot easier and healthier to use than sprays and chemicals.

PLANT

Foxglove

Digitalis purpureus

This tall spire of bell-shaped flowers, familiar to gardeners in the Northeast, is actually a native of Europe, where it was essential to peasants' pharmacopoeia. William Withering, a young eighteenth-century physician, loathed botany and the art of apothecary but desired to use his great knowledge of chemistry to treat maladies of the heart. Court physicians treated heart disease by bleeding and purging their patients, sometimes to death. Withering scoured the British countryside for the home remedies of midwives and folk healers who made up their own concoctions to treat coronary edema, then known as dropsy. Withering found that foxglove was the single common plant in every formula, and in his laboratory he isolated the compound that is still used today.

Our garden foxgloves are bold and beautiful hybrids available in a wider range of color than their original purple or mauve wild ancestor. Though far too toxic to use as a medicinal, foxglove remains an excellent shade-garden plant that evokes the accumulated wisdom of countless peasant healers.

Foxglove

Digitalis purpureus

Zone 3

Type: Perennial or biennial flowers

Origin: Europe

Habitat: Full sun or part shade in the south

Size: Foliage 12 to 14 inches tall, blooming to 5 feet

Plant: Spring or fall, from seed or containers

Notable feature: Extraordinary cutting flower

Lord, when I fall victim to the sin of vanity, believing that I have learned all I need to know, remind me that great mysteries remain in the world and in my garden. Keep my mind open to learning even on my final day of life, for this will keep me fully immersed in living. Amen.

God makes the earth yield healing herbs
        which the prudent man should not neglect;
Was not the water sweetened by a twig
        that men might learn his power?
He endows men with the knowledge
        to glory in his mighty works,
Through which the doctor eases pain
        and the druggist prepares his medicines;
Thus God's creative work continues without cease
        in its efficacy on the surface of the earth.

SIRACH 38:4–8

June

fourth week

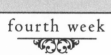

JUNE 21 SUMMER SOLSTICE

Meditation

The summer solstice, which is the day of the longest daytime, falls on or around June 21 in the Northern Hemisphere. It is a most auspicious date in terms of gathering healing herbs, and the solstice has traditionally played an important role in all sorts of folklore and tradition. There is solid science behind this association because plants recognize subtle changes in their environment far more than we do. The solstice ushers in the incremental shortening of days, which actually signals to plants that the period of vegetative growth has ended and it is time to get on with reproduction. This is particularly visible in the kitchen garden where the tomatoes, peppers, and squash come in earnest from this day forward. Similarly, medicinal herbs have built up their internal potency and if harvested now are most efficacious, but their potency will dwindle as they turn their attention toward flowering. These circumstances drew housewife healers and monks out into their gardens to gather their herbs on the solstice. The summer solstice is a great time to explore these Old World ways and read up on medicinal herbs that should be part of everyone's flower garden.

Benedict had laid down in the early sixth century that it was the duty of monks to care for the sick, and to do so as skillfully and intelligently as possible. Cassiodorus (487–583) urged the same responsibility on his monks: "Study with care the nature of herbs and the compoundings of drugs. If you have no knowledge of Greek, you have at hand the Herbarium of Dioscorides who fully described the flowers of the fields and illustrated them with drawings."

Barbara Griggs, *Green Pharmacy*, 1981

Gardening

Notice the surface of the soil, which in spring had been soft and crumbly to the touch. It is now likely a dry, hard crust that repels water quite well, leaving plants struggling to find moisture under this impenatrable surface. There are two ways to treat this problem. The first is to cultivate the soil and open it up to the air, which is a lot of work and must be repeated often as the dirt will harden after the first rainfall or watering. The second and more reasonable approach is to apply a protective covering of mulch.

Popular mulching materials range from ground fir bark to straw or even leaves saved from the previous autumn. After the soil is fully warmed, apply mulch in a layer about two inches thick. Mulch is not tilled into the soil but merely sits on top. This layer of mulch shades the soil, preventing the surface baking that sets up that hard crusty surface. Best of all, mulch blocks sunlight so that weed seeds do not sprout. You will be pleased to find that you need not water as often and that plants will cease to wilt in the hot afternoon sun.

PLANT

Apothecary Rose
Rosa gallica officinalis

Everyone who loves herbs and home remedies must grow at least one plant of *Rosa gallica*. In first-century Rome, Pliny the Elder wrote about its virtues and medicinal qualities. Starting in the sixth century, the apothecary rose was grown at thousands of Benedictine monasteries throughout Europe and was the most valuable rose in the Benedictine's medicinal pharmacy. While cultivation of this and many other old Roman species ceased during the

Middle Ages, these monasteries are credited with the preservation of countless strains.

The blood of this red rose flows in the veins of most modern roses, particularly the early hybrids. Once established, the apothecary rose will spread out underground and grow in thickets similar to blackberries, providing the home gardener with plenty of medicinal material. The apothecary rose is short in stature and makes a fine disease-free landscape shrub. Because it blooms but once a year, avoid pruning after the bloom season if you want a good-sized crop of rose-hip fruits. These roses are propagated in smaller numbers than the modern everblooming roses and sell out early, so be sure to order ahead or buy from the heritage rose sources in the back of this book.

Apothecary Rose

Rosa gallica officinalis

Zone 3

Type: Old rose species

Origin: Europe or Asia Minor

Habitat: Full sun

Size: 5 feet tall and as wide

Plant: Spring or fall, bare root or from containers

Notable feature: Highly fragrant, ancient medicinal species

Lord, help me to live according to the seasons of the sun. Thank you for making each day a little bit different, however slight its length may seem, so that living in the garden is a new experience each morning. Amen.

*I*t was once believed that God showed us which disorders certain plants cured by a plant's resemblance to the diseased part of the body. Known as the Doctrine of Signatures, it was based on the language in the passage from the Old Testament book of Sirach excerpted this week. For example, liverworts are small, flat, green plants about the size of a dime that cling to wet earth in colonies. Their slightly irregular shape was thought to resemble that of the human liver, so it was believed to cure liver disease. Many such cures are still recognized by herbalists even though they have no basis in fact or medicine.

June 24 Feast of St. John

Long ago, June 24 was designated as the summer solstice, which began the association of the solstice with St. John the Baptist. Another reason for the connection is based on John the Baptist's words about Christ: He must increase; I must decrease (John 3:30). This language came to represent the gradual increase of nighttime hours and the decrease of daylight hours from this point forward until the winter solstice. As a result, St. John the Baptist's day became integrated into many of the agrarian solstice customs of Europe and Britain.

This date connected St. John to *Hypericum perforatum,* a wild herb of the countryside that blooms bright yellow at this time of year. It was first named *Hypericum* by the Greeks, who hung it in their homes and temples as a protective plant. In the old pagan religions its sun-shaped yellow center was thought to protect against demons and enchantment, hence another old name: *Fuga daemonum.* The Old English name for plants was *wort,* so hypericum became St. John's plant, or St. Johnswort. This dedication to the saint was thought to make plants powerful, and their efficacy increased around the summer solstice when tiny red spots appear on the leaves. These were thought to be drops of the saint's blood from his beheading. It is not uncommon to still find fresh sprigs of the plant in houses and barns in rural Britain as protection against evil spirits, although the golden yellow flowers are more likely there for mere beauty.

Today the medicinal species of this plant, *Hypericum perforatum* (perforated St. Johnswort), is widely used as an herbal supplement to combat depression. The two species grown in American gardens are *Hypericum calycinum* and *Hypericum frondosum,* which are much more attractive ornamental plants. Consider planting *Hypericum* as a way to dedicate a small corner of your garden to this great man.

The Parson's wife prefers not the city, but her gardens and fields of hyssop, valerian, yarrow, and St. John's wort, which made into a poultice have done great and rare cures.

George Herbert, *Country Parson,* **seventeenth century**

St. Johnswort

Hypericum frondosum 'Sunburst'

Zone 4

Type: Flowering shrub

Origin: North America

Habitat: Full sun

Size: 3 feet tall and 4 feet wide

Plant: Spring or fall, from containers

July

Cattail
Typha latifolia
Zone 4
Type: Wetland reed
Origin: Waterways of North America, Europe, and Asia
Habitat: Full sun, water gardens
Size: 6 feet tall, spreading indefinitely
Plant: From containers
Notable feature: Decorative, cigar-shaped seed spikes

Bulrush, Cattail

Typha latifolia

The infant Moses was hidden in the bulrushes growing along the banks of the Nile. *Bulrush* is a general term for any number of large rushes or sedges that thrive in the shallows of the water's edge. The bulrushes that sheltered Moses were likely some combination of papyrus and cattails. Because the cattail is so common in low-lying, wet ground around the world, it has come to symbolize those of low social status who live lives of quiet Christian humility.

> "So I propose to build a temple in honor of the LORD, my God, as the LORD predicted to my father David when he said: 'It is your son whom I will put upon your throne in your place who shall build the temple in my honor.' Give orders, then, to have cedars from the Lebanon cut down for me. My servants shall accompany yours, since you know that there is no one among us who is skilled in cutting timber like the Sidonians, and I will pay you whatever you say for your servants' salary."
>
> 1 KINGS 5:19–20

July

JULY 1 BLESSED JUNÍPERO SERRA

Meditation

King Solomon built his temple with cedar because of the wood's unique and valuable qualities. Cedar is highly resistant to decomposition, symbolizing the eternity of God. The wood naturally repels insects, keeping the contents of a cedar chest permanently free of pests. Some considered the beautiful wood to be as valuable as gold—a fitting honor for God in both its beauty and richness. The book of 1 Kings describes the interior of the temple as wholly veneered in cedar and "showing no stone." The modern-day equivalent of this lavish display would be a gold-plated temple. Unfortunately, Solomon's relentless demand for cedar left few of the ancient giants standing, and we can now only imagine what those lofty groves must have looked like thousands of years ago.

Redwoods live long enough to awe the mind. A redwood has a normal life expectancy
of 1,000 to 1,500 years. The oldest specimen whose rings have been counted
is estimated to be 2,200 years old; a section of this log is preserved,
for the doubting, in the Richardson Grove, part of California's state park system.
So that tree began to grow when Hannibal was taking his elephants over the alps;
it was more than 200 years old at the birth of Jesus.

Donald Culross Peattie, *A Natural History of Western Trees,* **1950**

Gardening

In the heat of summer, trees can suffer from their own little drought, particularly if they are young with a still-small root system. Western states are accustomed to dry periods of six months or more, and trees will slow their growth or stop growing if not watered. The same can apply to regions that regularly receive summer rainfall but may be experiencing an unusually dry year. Keeping close watch on your trees for signs of dehydration is doubly important in hot windy weather.

The best way to hydrate trees is to water in a way that ensures that the moisture penetrates deep underground. One simple technique is to use a garden hose that is set just to a trickle. Place the hose at the base of the tree trunk and run the water overnight, which will allow it to seep well into the earth with no waste or evaporation. Deep watering is particularly beneficial to trees in lawns because the grass tends to suck up all the water before it can seep down into the tree root zone. If you give your trees a deep drink of water every week or two during a long hot summer, they will grow better and become less vulnerable to pests and diseases that strike weakened, dehydrated plants.

PLANT

Coast Redwood

Sequoia sempervirens

The redwood trees of the Pacific Coast are almost exclusively indigenous to California. There are only two species of redwood, *Sequoia sempervirens* and another found only in a very small part of the Sierra Nevada. This coast redwood, the one most often used in landscaping, is considered the tallest tree in the world. The largest coast redwood measured 334 feet tall with a diameter of over 21 feet. If you saw these trees in their natural habitat, you'd notice that they like to grow in clusters of many individuals. Their combined canopies shade a large area, which keeps their fibrous surface roots cool and moist under the litter of fallen leaves. It's odd that the largest trees on earth should have such a fine root system, but they feed right at the surface of the soil, just like a rhododendron, so that cultivating under the canopy or growing lawns there can interfere with their nutrient uptake. Cutting off the lower limbs, a common practice to allow mower access or to expose the trunk of redwoods that are

grown in landscapes, further slows growth, and as roots heat up in the sun the plants will prove far less resistant to drought. This tree is a beautiful example of why we need to understand how a tree grows in the wild if we are to provide it with the proper conditions in our gardens.

Coast Redwood

Sequoia sempervirens

Zone 7

Type: Evergreen conifer tree

Origin: California

Habitat: Full sun

Size: 60 to 70 feet tall and 25 to 30 feet wide

Plant: Anytime, from containers

Lord, although Solomon honored you with a great temple of cedar trees, it did not last. Remind me that your temple on earth lies exclusively in the hearts of your people, not in their buildings or treasure. Let me celebrate and care for each human being and every living tree as a creation that manifests your love. Amen.

Redwood of the Franciscans

The sons of St. Francis followed the Spanish conquistadors into the New World to found missions among the indigenous people. Once missions were established in Mexico, various expeditions traveled north into the vast wilderness of the American West known as Alta California. Father Juan Crespi was the first European to describe the legendary redwood trees while on the Portolá expedition in 1769. "They [the redwoods] have a very different leaf from cedars, and although the wood resembles cedar somewhat in color, it is very different and has not the same odor." In 1776 Father Pedro Font, on the d'Anza expedition—the first Western sighting of the San Francisco Bay—wrote of seeing "a few spruce trees which they call redwood, a tree that is certainly very useful for its timber." The wood of these trees was discovered to be highly resistant to rot, even more so than cedar. It was used for all sorts of construction within its range, particularly foundations in the mission communities. When he was near death, Bl. Junipero Serra, the father of the missions, asked to be buried in a redwood coffin at Mission San Carlos Borromeo at Carmel. He was buried in 1784 under the church, but in 1852 the long abandoned mission collapsed and the grave was never relocated. Nearly two hundred years after his burial, when the mission was undergoing restoration, Serra's coffin was found perfectly intact. The trees that the Franciscans discovered served them well, for their wood not only preserved the great mission churches but also cradled the remains of the holiest man of early California.

Jesus said to them, "My food is to do the will of the one who sent me and to finish his work. Do you not say, 'In four months the harvest will be here'? I tell you, look up and see the fields ripe for the harvest. The reaper is already receiving his payment and gathering crops for eternal life, so that the sower and reaper can rejoice together. For here the saying is verified that 'One sows and another reaps.' I sent you to reap what you have not worked for; others have done the work, and you are sharing the fruits of their work."

JOHN 4:34–38

July

Meditation

When the garden begins to mature this time of year, everyone who neglected their spring chores scrambles to get plants and seeds into the ground. The nurseries have sold out of the best varieties, and what remains is undoubtedly pot-bound. The weather has grown too hot for tender seedlings. This failure to plan ahead—to start seeds indoors, to fortify and till the soil, and to get the garden in order—means no harvest, no new potatoes or early tender squash. In a way it is the same with our spiritual life, for if we don't study our faith, if we don't practice the art of prayer or attend Mass weekly, we will have little to harvest. When the struggles of life heat up to intolerable levels, our lean spiritual gardens will not sustain us. Sadly, many people discover too late that they are ill prepared, and they struggle to catch up under a withering summer sun.

Gardening

This is the month when the kitchen garden is growing at its fastest pace and the plants require greater attention. Potatoes planted in hills will produce spuds at a shallow depth around the stem and only occasionally will spuds grow directly beneath the stem. Therefore, as the tubers grow larger they pop out of the top of the soil and, exposed to sunlight, promptly turn green. To protect these surface spuds and ensure that each of them matures properly, try "hilling up." Build little mounds of fresh earth around the maturing plant. Where little earth is available, a thick mulch of straw is sufficient to keep the sun out. This month in cooler climates you'll find "new" potatoes in the upper part of the root zone, and if you reach inside the mound you can harvest a few for a summer morning breakfast without damage to the plant. There is no comparison between the flavor of freshly dug potatoes and potatoes from the supermarket, making this a rare delicacy known only to those who had the foresight to sow their potatoes.

PLANT

Purple Potato

Solanum ajanhuiri

Kitchen gardeners rarely sow the standard red, white, or russet supermarket potato varieties. Thanks to a growing interest in gourmet potato varieties you can now buy seed potatoes for dozens of different heirloom varieties. These include the wonderful "fingerling" types, which are ideal for small gardens. But the best of all are the purple Peruvian potatoes—our closest link to the original potato strains grown in the Incan gardens of the Andes centuries ago. The conquistadors introduced them to Europe, where they were sometimes called the truffle potato because of their rich nutty flavor.

The skin of the *Solanum ajanhuiri* is eggplant purple on the outside and the flesh is various shades of lavender or is white with purple or lavender stripes. These are great potatoes to roast for a uniquely beautiful dish. Good quality, disease-free purple seed potatoes can be purchased through the mail from suppliers listed in the back of this book. The plants are quite disease resistant, surviving where white potatoes will die out.

Purple Potato

Solanum ajanhuiri

All zones

Type: Seasonal root crop

Origin: South America

Habitat: Full sun

Size: 2 feet tall and 2 to 3 feet wide

Plant: Spring, from seed potatoes

Notable feature: Edible tubers with purple flesh

All-powerful God, we appeal to your tender care that even as you temper the winds and rains to nurture the fruits of the earth, you will also send upon them the gentle shower of your blessing. Fill the hearts of your people with gratitude, that from the earth's fertility the hungry may be filled with good things, and the poor and needy proclaim the glory of your name. Amen.

From Roman Ritual Book of Blessings, *by the International Commission on English in the Liturgy*

In Ireland, the important dates for sowing and harvesting were coordinated with the Catholic calendar. Early planting began on St. Patrick's Day. The only work on Good Friday was the late sowing of potatoes, for it was thought that as Jesus was buried so should these tubers be. July is the month of potato harvest, and in Galway, harvest begins on Garland Sunday, the same date as the old pre-Christian feast of first fruits, Lughnasa. In Kerry, harvest begins on the feast of the local patron, St. Palladius, on July 7.

Praise the LORD from the earth,

      you sea monsters and all deep waters; . . .

You mountains and all hills,

      fruit trees and all cedars;

You animals wild and tame,

      you creatures that crawl and fly;

You kings of the earth and all peoples,

      princes and all who govern on earth;

Young men and women too,

      old and young alike.

Let them all praise the Lord's name.

PSALM 148:7–13

third week

Meditation

All gardeners, farmers, and even naturalists share a deep-seated belief that there is divinity in the earth. Each person will harbor a different image of that divinity, which will manifest itself according to that person's field of knowledge, be it plants, animals, weather, or all of these. Some find traces of the divine in the remarkable tenacity of weeds or in the life sequestered through the winter in what would appear a dead stick or root. This great sense of a higher power behind it all extends to the miracles of wildlife— discovering a swallowtail butterfly on valerian flowers or admiring weaver- birds that are born with the ability to create the complex architecture of their pendulous nests. Even in the sometimes tumultuous weather of this season, with its spectacle of summer lightning and the occasional tornado, there is awesome beauty. The psalmist clearly recognizes that all things on earth acknowledge God, their creator, with their very existence, and that we too may find this wonder a continuous inspiration in all that surrounds us. Too many take it for granted, but finding that childlike sense of wonder in all that is will surely lead us to heaven.

Gardening

The oppressive July heat that drives us indoors or into the shade marks a time when many wild things are thriving and feeding their young. It is important to encourage those beneficial living things to flourish so that they prey successfully on the unwanted pests in our garden. Birds are among our most vigorous biopesticides because they prey on the fat hornworms that munch our tomatoes and on the armyworms that love the marigolds. Birds will linger in our garden longer if we provide them with a pool of clean water in which to cool their feathers. Create numerous birdbaths around the garden with economical large clay saucers about eighteen inches in diameter. Set these saucers on a stump or any other perch and see them draw birds all day. These simple water sources attract colorful butterflies and even appeal to wasps, which despite their sting are also valuable caterpillar predators. Be sure to provide a comfortable seat for yourself in the midst of all of this so that you may quietly rediscover that childlike sense of wonder as this divine plan unfolds before you.

PLANT

Hybrid Bearded Iris

Iris hybrids

Bearded iris are among the most gorgeous and resilient flowers in any garden. They originated in Europe as hybrids in the seventeenth century, but it wasn't until the late Victorian era, when bedding perennials were in demand, that the flush of new cultivars appeared. Unlike any other flowers, these grow from fleshy roots that sit just at the surface of the soil, a valuable trait for gardens with difficult, rocky, or shallow soil. Iris are well adapted to virtually any climate, thriving in the colder north and the hot, dry west with little to no water over the summer months. Their long bloom season extends from early spring until the onset of summer heat. It's at this time, from July onward, after flowering has ceased, that irises are best divided and spread throughout the garden. Simply lift out the network of rhizomes with a spading fork, taking care not to stab the fleshy parts. Then break the segments apart at the natural joints so that each growing point is provided with a single, good-sized segment of its own. Allow them to dry out a day or two to prevent rotting, and then replant, shallowly, wherever there is adequate drainage and plentiful sun.

Bearded Iris

Iris hybrids

Zone 3

Type: Perennial flower

Origin: Europe

Habitat: Full sun

Size: Ranges from a 10-inch-tall dwarf to 28-inch-tall varieties

Plant: Spring or fall, bare root or from containers

Lord, help me to remember that all living things are part of an intricate, divine plan. In your wisdom you have created a world in which all things are connected—from the thunderhead clouds of summer to the rich earth beneath my feet. Let the hours I spend in the garden bring me closer to each of the elements and to you as their creator. Amen.

He proposed another parable to them. "The kingdom of heaven is like a mustard seed that a person took and sowed in a field. It is the smallest of all the seeds, yet when full-grown it is the largest of plants. It becomes a large bush, and the 'birds of the sky come and dwell in its branches.'"

MATTHEW 13:31–32

JULY 31 FEAST OF ST. IGNATIUS OF LOYOLA

Meditation

The parable of the mustard seed provides us with a beautiful analogy for the legacy of St. Ignatius. His order of missionary priests, the Society of Jesus, was founded in 1540 and began to spread the gospel around the world. This tiny seed of their early efforts grew into many great, though not widely known, contributions to horticultural history. While in their often remote missions, many Jesuits explored their surroundings and discovered for the West new plants and animals. Spanish Jesuits in the New World were responsible for the discovery of the *Cinchona* tree and the quinine derived from its bark. Their discovery has saved millions of lives. Jesuits also contributed corn, tomatoes, and peppers to the European diet, staving off starvation and disease.

French Jesuits in China supplied the botanical gardens of Paris with hundreds of new species. Missionaries in this remote field shared their plant collections with British explorers working for Kew Gardens in the nineteenth century. The explorers would often take credit for the discoveries themselves when introducing them into English language botanical references. Meanwhile, the humble Jesuit botanists remained in the field, unrecognized for their valuable efforts. Fortunately, the archives of Europe kept records of the Jesuits' contributions, which include pressed plants, detailed drawings, and extensive letters that document their very important works.

During this period—the middle decades of the seventeenth century—the Jesuits in China were encouraged to show off all their talents. They built fountains and mechanical toys, laid out ornamental gardens; "it suddenly began to seem," writes the historian Rene Fulop-Miller, "as if the Society of Jesus was a guild of painters and architects, and Christianity merely an esoteric branch of landscape gardening."

Manfred Barthel, *The Jesuits: History and Legend of the Society of Jesus*, 1984,
translated by Mark Howson

Gardening

Like the invisible human soul, the roots of a plant are deep underground, hidden from view. When you plant a tree or shrub from a nursery container, its roots are at first confined to the shape of that pot. During the first summer in your garden, the plant will be able to draw moisture and nutrients from only this limited area, and with the onset of summer heat, this limitation may cause it to suffer. Even if you were to water the plant frequently, the water may flow around the compact root ball without penetrating it, and when the center dries out, the plant will invariably die by season's end.

If you see such signs of dryness as wilting leaves or out-of-season leaf drop, you must not just water but soak the root ball itself. Set the garden hose at the base of the plant's trunk or stem and allow it to trickle for a while. This water will move straight down into the center of the root ball to hydrate the roots from the inside out. Repeat this each time you see signs of need over this first crucial summer, and be sure to add a covering of mulch to keep the ground cool and reduce surface evaporation.

PLANT

Peruvian Lily

Alstromeria ligtu hybrid

The beautiful flowers of *Alstromeria* are well known to the florist, but less well known is their surprising resiliency as garden perennials in warmer climates. Their story can be traced back to a traveling French Jesuit, Louis Econches Feuilee. While traveling through central Chile in 1791, he collected the seed and described it in his journals as a New World daylily. He called it *ligtu* after the local name for the plant, and he brought it back to Europe and gave the seeds to botanist Claus Alstromer, then living in Spain. Alstromer named it *Econches* after the priest. They were then forwarded on to Carolus Linnaeus, who was so taken with the flowers he nursed them through a cold northern winter in his bedroom! He classified it in his *Species Plantarum* (1762) as genus and species *Alstromeria ligtu*. Sadly this left the name of poor Feuilee out of the picture altogether. It was not until 1870 that these fabulous plants were bred by Belgian Louis Van Houtte to create the hybrid grown today. *Alstromeria* is a bedding perennial that does best in the South and West and is not hardy outdoors north of Philadelphia. They do, however, grow well in containers and may be potted up at the end of the season to overwinter indoors just as they did so successfully for Linnaeus.

Peruvian Lily

Alstromeria hybrids

Zone 8

Type: Perennial flower

Origin: South America

Habitat: Full sun in cooler climates, part shade elsewhere

Size: 3 to 4 feet tall, clumping as wide

Plant: Anytime, from containers

Teach us, good Lord, to serve you as you deserve:
To give and not to count the cost;
To fight and not to heed the wounds;
To toil and not to seek for rest;
To labor and not to ask for any reward
Save that of knowing that we do your will.
　　　　　　　　　—St. Ignatius Loyola, Prayer for Generosity

He would become one of the greatest French botanists of Asia, and his name would fill horticultural references despite the fact that many of his discoveries would be claimed by others. Jean Marie Delavay entered the priesthood through the Society of Foreign Missions and found himself in the Kwangtung province of China in 1867. When he was not preaching or serving his converts, the abbé began to hike the unknown wilderness around his mission in northwest Yunnan to collect and classify more new plants than any of his European contemporaries. His specimens were regularly sent back to Adrien Franchet of the Jardin des Plantes in Paris.

Over a ten-year period, Delavay explored much of Yunnan and the Hupeh and Szechwan provinces as well. In 1888 he was attacked by plague and sent home to France. Though partially paralyzed from his illness, he insisted on returning to China, where he died soon after in 1895.

Delavay is credited with the discovery and classification of many heavy-scented flowering plants, notably the fragrant pink jasmine *Jasminum polyanthum* and *Magnolia delavayi,* which is well known in American gardens today. He is also the source of *Osmanthus delavayi,* the sweet-scented osmanthus that he found growing in Chinese temple grounds, where the fragrance was considered an offering to their gods.

Delavay is also credited with introducing two species of peony to the West, *Paeonia delavayi* and *Paeonia lutea,* which gave the French the leading edge in European peony breeding. Other introductions include trees such as Delavay's fir, *Abies delavayi, Ligusticum delavayi,* and richly scented star jasmine, *Trachelospermum jasminoides.* This devoted priest would discover more than thirty new species of *Rhododendron,* which first grew in France but would later be rediscovered and credited to the English explorers working for Kew, the nursery firm of Veitch & Sons, and the Royal Horticultural Society.

*T*he hot days of late summer that begin about the second week of July, and in ancient times began with the rising of the Little Dog Star Canicula—from the Latin word *canis*—were first referred to as the "dog days" by the Romans. Dog days have since become an expression for these warm, languid days during late summer.

August

Wormwood

Artemisia absinthum

Zone 8

Type: Perennial herb

Origin: Europe

Habitat: Full sun

Size: 2 to 4 feet tall and as wide

Plant: Spring or fall, from containers

Notable feature: Aromatic herb, natural pesticide

Wormwood

Artemisia absinthum

Wormwood, a strongly aromatic plant closely related to American sagebrush, has a distinctly bitter taste, which led to its use as a biblical symbol for sorrow and disaster. The gall offered to Christ just before his death is believed to have been wormwood, which was given to dying criminals to alleviate their suffering. Because of its role in the Crucifixion, wormwood is believed to be blessed, and sprigs of it were often hung in the household as protection.

Who has laid out a channel for the downpour
      and for the thunderstorm a path
To bring rain to no man's land,
      the unpeopled wilderness;
To enrich the waste and desolate ground
      till the desert blooms with verdure?

Job 38: 25–27

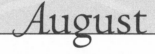

August

Meditation

The American prairie reaches its zenith in this latter part of the summer. Watered by violent thunderstorms, millions of acres of grasslands span our continent. In places, we can drive through these grasslands for hours without encountering another soul. Similarly, we find the deserts of the West a near identical environment, where the simplicity of earth and sky seems so insistent that experiencing it drives out all complexity from our life for awhile. For those who live a frenetic city life, the emptiness of this wilderness landscape, what in Montana is called "big sky country," is an antidote to urban sensory assault. No sounds but the wind and the rustling of the grasses, with their tall seed heads swaying in the breezes, the scent of sagebrush in the air, and the sight of wildflowers in bloom all around us. Like the desert fathers, it is time to go into the wilderness and rediscover ourselves.

*There is perhaps no nature-study that can yield the same amount of pure and
unalloyed pleasure with so little outlay as the study of wild flowers.
When one is interested in them, every walk into the fields is transformed
from an aimless ramble into a joyous, eager quest, and every journey upon stage
or railroad becomes a rare opportunity for making new plant acquaintances—
a season of exhilarating excitement.*

Mary Elizabeth Parsons, *The Wild Flowers of California*, 1902

Gardening

Wildflowers are just that, plants that grow as wild as the weeds and bloom
their hearts out each year. The annual wildflowers are fickle fellows, and
if you sowed seed this spring you likely enjoyed a beautiful stand. If you
did not cut it back after flowers faded you may expect a showing next year,
but it will likely be disappointing. Unless plants go to seed and that seed
finds conditions over winter and spring acceptable, they simply won't germinate. In the wild, annuals are very picky about where they choose to
dwell, and the suitability of any particular site is told by the flush of color
year after year.

Perennial wildflowers are far more reliable than annuals, and some have
become very popular garden plants as a result. They are planted from
seedlings grown in a nursery. A successful perennial may be divided into
many new plants after a few years, making them economical in the long
run. Your native perennial wildflowers, such as coneflower, penstemon, lia-
tris, coreopsis, and evening primrose, slow down in the late summer heat,
but keep tending them for healthier plants next year. Cut back their faded
flowers so they do not expend valuable growth energy on seed production.
Provide plenty of water and mild fertilizer to encourage an expanded root
system, which guarantees more blooms next summer.

PLANT

Purple Coneflower

Echinacea purpurea

This striking magenta-pink flowering perennial hails from the tallgrass prairie of the Midwest and is at its best in mid to late summer. It is heat and cold hardy, growing in a huge range from northern Michigan south to Louisiana. Its name is derived from the center of its daisy flower, which expands into an attractive, egg-sized, cone-shaped seed structure. Bees and butterflies are drawn to the flowers of this plant, which makes it a fixture in every butterfly garden. Later, the seed heads attract birds.

Coneflowers develop into big clumps by the second or third year and are naturally drought and disease resistant. Although it is called purple, the flowers of this plant are really more pink, with the white cultivar 'White Swan' giving gardeners another option.

The root of the purple coneflower was used as medicine by Native Americans, and echinacea is gaining prominence as an herbal supplement that stimulates the immune system. Buy your cone-flowers as seedlings from a reputable nursery. Never pick, dig up, or damage these plants in the wild. Overharvesting has caused them to become rare or disappear altogether from many wild places where they were once plentiful.

Purple Coneflower

Echinacea purpurea

Zone 4

Type: Flowering perennial

Origin: Midwestern prairie

Habitat: Full sun

Size: 3 feet tall, spreading to 4 or 5 feet wide

Plant: Spring or fall, from containers

Notable feature: Attracts butterflies

Lord, as the thunderstorms of late summer roll across the land, make me mindful of the way it was here in America before settlers plowed the prairies. Through wildflowers grant me visions of blooming desert, grass-cloaked plains, tree-shrouded mountains. I know the face of the land may change, but its plants will tell its story forever. Amen.

An ancient Celtic legend says that daisies represent the spirits of children who died at birth. God sprinkled these bright and lovely flowers across the earth to cheer the grieving parents.

> "When you have come into the land which the LORD, your God, is giving you as a heritage, and have occupied it and settled in it, you shall take some first fruits of the various products of the soil which you harvest from the land which the LORD, your God, gives you, and putting them in a basket, you shall go to the place which the LORD, your God, chooses for the dwelling place of his name."
>
> DEUTERONOMY 26:1–2

August

Meditation

This month the kitchen garden is in high gear, and summer-blooming flowers are everywhere. First Fruits is a day when the farmers of Israel brought the first of their harvest to the temple to be given to the priests or to be sacrificed. The significance of this sacrifice is lost on modern-day supermarket shoppers. Throughout the spring and early summer, little if any grain would have been left from the year before, which meant that bread would have been scarce. The first grain harvested was given up to God at a time when the body's craving for carbohydrates was overwhelming. Only after the offerings at the start of the harvest did farmers quickly grind the wheat to bake those first fragrant loaves.

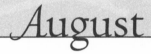

At this time of year our sweet tomatoes are plentiful, savory summer squash go onto the grill, and the corn is ripe. As we enjoy the first fruits of our garden, let us make an act of thanksgiving. Bring your most perfect flowers to the dwelling place of his name and place them as an offering before Jesus or

Mary. To give them up to God is a beautiful act that will link your garden to our Lord in a deeply meaningful way.

Through gardening we are given so many more opportunities to thank God. When we taste the first fruit of each tree or vegetable, the shehechiyanu, *which is the prayer of thanksgiving said when doing something for the first time or for the first time in the present season, gives us a simple, direct way to interact with God. Because we went through the whole process—sowing, tending, and harvesting—the "thanks" means so much more than it would for produce that has been grown by someone in a different state, or even halfway around the world.*

Michael P. Brown, *The Jewish Gardening Cookbook,* **1998**

Gardening

An annual plant must sprout, mature, flower, and produce seed for next year within just one short growing season. The presence of seed signals the plant to cease flowering because it has accomplished its job of reproduction. This fact is very important for both flower and vegetable gardening because fruit must be picked promptly in order to keep the plant in flower and producing more fruit. With squash, for example, if you pick your young, soft fruit daily or every other day, the plant will produce more fruit than if you allow that zucchini to grow to the size of a football. To maximize your yields, go out and pick flowers and veggies every day, whether you need them or not. Prompt harvesting is vital to peas, beans, tomatoes, peppers, and eggplant. It is also essential to water these hardworking veggies well during these dog days of summer so their growth does not slow for lack of sustenance.

PLANT

Tomato

Lycopersicon esculentum

Can you imagine Italian cuisine without the tomato? You may be surprised to discover it was wholly absent until Columbus introduced plants from the New World to Europe. However, the tomato was considered a potentially poisonous member of the nightshade family, and Europeans dared not taste the fruit. It remained a *planta non grata* in Europe and even much of North America until the late nineteenth century, when science finally revealed the virtues of the tomato. Since then dozens of varieties have been produced from the early heirlooms, which are no longer grown commercially.

It is important to know whether a garden tomato is determinate or indeterminate. Determinate varieties, used in commercial agriculture and home canning, are grown in short-season climates because the whole crop ripens at once. Indeterminate varieties bloom and fruit repeatedly over a very long season, extending the harvest of fresh tomatoes for your kitchen. Another tip for success with tomatoes is that unlike all other vegetables, they will produce roots wherever stem contacts the earth. Plant tomato seedlings in a deep hole to provide for a much larger root system and stronger plants overall.

Tomatoes are the seductive vegetable—bright red, bursting with juice and flavor, fruitful to a fault. Had they been native not to Peru but to Asia Minor, a tomato—not an apple—would surely have caused our fall from grace.

Barbara Damrosch,
The Garden Primer, 1988

Tomato

Lycopersicon lycopersicum
All zones
Type: Seasonal crop
Origin: Central America
Habitat: Full sun
Size: Variable
Plant: After last frost, from seed or containers
Notable feature: Popular edible fruit/vegetable

Say when offering your flowers at church or home shrine . . .
Lord, please accept the humble offering of these flowers from my garden. Though I planted and tended them, I know you gave them life and that I merely acted as caretaker. May their beauty be a sign of my devotion to you. Amen.

Listen to a man of experience: thou wilt learn more in the woods than in books.

St. Bernard of Clairvaux, Epistle 106

Filled with the holy Spirit, Jesus returned from the Jordan and was led by the Spirit into the desert for forty days, to be tempted by the devil. He ate nothing during those days, and when they were over he was hungry. The devil said to him, "If you are the Son of God, command this stone to become bread." Jesus answered him, "It is written, 'One does not live by bread alone.'"

Luke 4:1–4

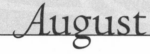

August

third week

August 20 Feast of St. Bernard of Clairvaux

Meditation

The writings of Thomas Merton have inspired seekers of every spiritual path and sometimes even those of no religious persuasion whatsoever. Merton was a twentieth-century Trappist monk who wrote many famous works, including the classic *Seven Story Mountain* about his life, conversion, and his eventual vocation. The Trappists lead a contemplative communal life of silence, prayer, and work. They seek to be as self-sufficient as possible, which requires that they do a great deal of rugged outdoor living in tending their fields, orchards, and livestock. These men are the legacy of St. Bernard of Clairvaux, who founded the Cistercian order in France nearly a millennium ago. Like Jesus, who spent forty days alone in the desert surrounded by nature, these Trappists live an outdoor life of simplicity and solitude.

The first Trappist monastery in America was founded in 1848 in Kentucky. It was known as Gesthemani. Since then, other abbeys have been founded all across the United States. Many of them provide rooms for guests, so if you wish to experience this agricultural monastic life firsthand, visit their Web site at www.cistercian-usa.org for more information.

*A tree gives glory to God first of all by being a tree. For in being what God means
it to be, it is imitating an idea which is in God and which is not distinct from the
essence of God, and therefore a tree imitates God by being a tree....
Unlike the animals and the trees, it is not enough for us to be individual men.
For us, holiness is more than humanity. If we are never anything but men,
never anything but our natural selves, we will not be saints and we will not be
able to offer to God the worship of our imitation, which is sanctity.*

Thomas Merton, *Seeds of Contemplation*, 1949

Gardening

Beautiful flowering vines are among the most valuable of all landscape plants. With these, nature cloaks all that is bare and ugly in a forgiving blanket of flowers and foliage. Vines, like people, require strict training while young to ensure they do not grow in the wrong direction, then regular attention throughout their lives to keep them from growing astray. It is essential you not allow vines to grow into the eaves of a house or garage because tendrils that access small gaps in the architecture can cause severe structural damage in the future.

This time of year some of these vines grow rampantly, with each new runner green and highly flexible. If promptly tied in position now, these runners will remain in place as they mature into rigid wood. Use flat-head galvanized nails to give the runners something to grab on to. If the wood structure that your vine is attached to is soft, try using wood screws with an eye, which will give them a secure structure. First tie your green plant tape or wire securely to the nail with a strong knot. Then when you train the runner, tie it down so that you've given it a little "play," which will allow the runner to move with the breeze and the plant to grow larger in diameter. Use as many anchors as necessary to secure the young runner without undue pressure on a single point, where it may break under stress.

PLANT

Trumpet Creeper

Campsis radicans

The big vibrant red and yellow clusters of huge trumpet flowers look as though they should come from some tropical jungle, but actually they are native to North America. This remarkable vine is hardy to zone 4, making it well suited to most climates. It is actually native to many of the eastern states, from New York south to Florida, and west to Texas, where its climbing aerial rootlets give it a foothold into the treetops of forested areas. Very early on, it became a mainstay of cottage gardens throughout the region, growing to a whopping 35 feet and self-seeding wherever possible. This size and fast growth are both a benefit and a liability as it can engulf a small yard if not controlled. It is virtually free of pests and disease, attracts hummingbirds, and blooms all summer long and well into the fall.

Trumpet Creeper

Campsis radicans

Zone 4

Type: Deciduous flowering vine

Origin: Southeastern United States

Habitat: Full sun

Size: Spreading to 25 or 30 feet

Plant: Spring or fall, from containers

Notable feature: Draws hummingbirds

Lord, my garden would not be beautiful without you.
My garden would not give me peace without you.
My garden would not be a creation without you.
The world would not be beautiful without you. Amen.

Until the spirit from on high
　　　is poured out on us.
Then will the desert become an orchard
　　　and the orchard be regarded as a forest.

Right will dwell in the desert
　　　and justice abide in the orchard.
Justice will bring about peace;
　　　right will produce calm and security.

ISAIAH 32:15–17

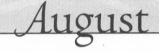 *August*

fourth week

AUGUST 30 FEAST OF ST. FIACRE, PATRON OF GARDENERS

Meditation

Although he is widely recognized in France for miracles he performed there in his later life, St. Fiacre, patron of gardeners, was a Celtic Christian. He was born in Ireland in 1590, the son of a pagan warrior-king who, because he was a druid, believed that the gods or spirits inhabited plants, making them sacred. This instilled in the boy a reverence for the green world, although his mother, a Christian, raised him in her own faith. He entered monastic life in France so that he might live as a hermit in the woods.

The Bishop of Meaux offered the ascetic Fiacre as much of an overgrown woodland as the monk could clear in a short time. Varying accounts claim that Fiacre miraculously cleared an enormous area with the help of God. Some say that angels felled the trees and pulled the plow. St. Fiacre planted his garden in the wilderness with herbs that he used to treat the ailing bodies of the poor, while he fed their souls as a confessor and counselor. He often prayed aloud to the Virgin Mary while tending his garden, always speaking to her in his native tongue, Gaelic. The monk worked all his life in the garden, which surely brought him good health, for he lived for eighty years—an incredible age when life expectancy was only half that.

*Those who labor in the earth are the chosen people of God, if ever He had
a chosen people, whose breasts He has made His peculiar deposit for substantial
and genuine virtue. It is the focus in which He keeps alive that sacred fire, which
otherwise might escape from the face of the earth.*

Thomas Jefferson

Gardening

There is no reason why your warm-season annual flowers shouldn't bloom continuously until frost, yet too many of us back off on care at summer's end. While annuals should get extra attention now, it's best to leave alone those other types of plants that must winter over, because stimulating them now can make them much more vulnerable to winter cold damage.

Because annuals live just for the immediate growing season, you can push them to the limit in the fall. Follow a few basic rules of annual color gardening that apply throughout the season but are particularly important now when plants sense the amount of daylight is decreasing. First, such flowers as marigolds and petunias work hard and, like human athletes, they need a steady, high-quality diet to keep them performing well. Make it a practice to use a liquid fertilizer, such as Miracle-Gro, every three weeks throughout the growing season to stimulate steady blooming in annual plants. Second, you must deadhead, or keep spent flower heads picked off the plants, so that the flower heads do not have a chance to set seed, which can further slow down flower production. Third, water deeply and on a regular basis, because in the hot, dry days of late summer and fall, plants can become stressed if not moistened. Plants can only fully utilize the fertilizer you give them if they are sufficiently watered. Finally, keep plant foliage free of accumulated dust, which promotes spider-mite infestation and reduces photosynthesis. Syringe plants with a strong jet of water from the garden hose once a week, preferably in early morning or late evening to avoid sunburn. Follow these tips, and when the other gardens are going to seed, yours will be going strong.

Sunflower

Helianthus annuus

Sunflowers are one of the most beloved plants in country gardens. They originated in the Midwest, and Native American women cultivated them for centuries on the flood plains of great rivers of the Midwest. These women domesticated the sunflower gradually by careful seed selection, increasing the size of the blossom to make the sunflowers more abundant food producers. From those original prairie flowers came the astounding 'Mammoth' sunflower, which produces seed heads the size of dinner plates! The flower bud faces the sun and will follow it across the sky, changing positions throughout the day. Only when the flower bud opens does the head become stationary. You can make sunflowers grow into a large bush by cutting off the head when young, which forces side branches to form. Each branch will produce a large number of smaller flowers that are great for cutting. Although 'Mammoth' and its short-stature cousins are commercial food crops, literally dozens of different sunflower varieties are just as easy to grow from seed. Explore the 'Prado Red' sunflowers, the amber orange, and the fancy shaggy 'Lions Mane'; or consider the Native American heirloom plants from the upper Midwest sold through Seeds of Change, or those of the desert Southwest sold through Native Seeds/SEARCH—both are listed in the resource section of this book. Be sure to give your sunflowers plenty of water and fertilizer throughout the year to produce big, prolific plants. Let the flowers go to seed, and wild birds will entertain you as they feed before migrating in the fall.

Sunflower

Helianthus annuus hybrids

All zones

Type: Annual flower

Origin: North America

Habitat: Full sun

Size: Varies from dwarf to mammoth varieties

Plant: Spring, from seed

Notable feature: Edible seeds

Lord, please help me to remain as strong and healthy as a sunflower by working in my garden. Give me a long life that I might become wise through the lessons of nature. And when I grow old, open up the furrows before me so that I need not work too hard. Above all, grant me the ability to work in my garden to my very last day so that I may never be separated from the flowers and earth I love. Amen.

*I*n Russia, the people abstained from a detailed list of fats and oils during Lent. Because the list was compiled before the sunflower was introduced into Russia, this oil was exempt. Widespread cultivation of the plants gave the people a Lenten "loophole" and a welcome addition to their sparse meals.

September

Grape

Vitis table hybrids
Zone 4 (*Vitis labrusca* hybrids)
Zone 7 (*Vitis vinifera* hybrids)
Origin: Mediterranean
Habitat: Full sun
Size: 20 to 25 feet
Plant: Spring or fall, bare root or
from containers
Notable feature: Edible fruit,
autumn color

Grape

Vitis vinifera

The grapevine is referred to in the Bible more than any other plant. Farmers

were cultivating the grapevine extensively in the Holy Land for millennia

before Christ, and he would use it to symbolize Christianity, with

himself as the trunk and the branches as the church. And it was from

the grapevine that wine was pressed, which Jesus offered as his

blood at the Last Supper. The grapevine is an essential fruit of the

desert—it offers food and wine, and it grows easily on arbors so that

gardeners could provide plentiful shade.

Be patient, therefore, brothers, until the coming of the Lord. See how the farmer waits for the precious fruit of the earth, being patient with it until it receives the early and the late rains.

JAMES 5:7

September

Meditation

It is said that a person does not come to gardening until at least the age of forty. Why? Because plants grow slowly and patience is needed to grow a garden. Remember when you were child and the cycle of the year seemed to last forever? At that age we wanted life to move at ever greater speeds; plants were too gradual to hold our interest. As we age, our sense of that annual span of time grows shorter and shorter. The slowness of plant growth becomes a comfort that helps to hold back the speed of life.

We can be thankful that aging makes us better gardeners. We aren't so impatient, and we will savor the wait for the tulips to bloom or for our trees to take on their autumn color. We are better at planning ahead. We are more organized and will take pains to accomplish a task deliberately and to a certain degree of completeness or perfection. We gardeners are blessed, and while tending this collection of living things we are rewarded with time to contemplate our unique role in our little patch of the universe.

The farmer should remember that every tree, shrub, and flower he cultivates constitutes a new link of attachment to bind him to his home, and render that home more delightful. They multiply our means of enjoyment, they make additions to our stock of knowledge, they invite us to a more intimate communion with nature, and they prevent the concentration of the mind on wealth, and the narrow selfishness that is too often its attendant.

Cultivator, vol. 9, "The Garden," 1842

Gardening

Planning is imperative for gardeners, particularly when it comes to planting spring bulbs. In September, spring bulbs go on sale, and they are everywhere. You must get them into the ground soon if you are to have a spring garden. A bulb is actually a little package of food energy that fuels the plant so that it may grow and bloom. After flowers fade, never cut off the remaining leaves. You must water and fertilize the bulb until the leaves die back on their own. This time after flowering is when the plant stores food energy in the bulb necessary for next year's flowers. If you fail to care for the plant or remove the leaves necessary for this process, the bulb will starve and either fail to bloom or simply die out altogether. For a really beautiful showing in spring, buy lots of bulbs in each color you choose so that the mass is clearly visible in the landscape. Hand-selected bulbs in open bins are usually of better quality than those already packaged in bags. Buy early so you can pick through them and choose the largest, most perfect bulbs of the lot.

PLANT

Hybrid Tulips

Tulipa Darwin hybrids

At least 2,500 different species and varieties of tulips are grown today in a wide range of sizes, colors, and unique flower shapes. Most are sold simply by their color, and the bigger the bulb, the better your flowers will be. Tulip hybrids come in virtually all colors of the rainbow except blue. Many are striped bicolors, which are quite showy when viewed close up.

These flowers are remarkably affordable and easy to grow, considering their singular beauty. The bulbs should be planted in the fall at an average depth of 6 to 12 inches in light, well-drained soil. Tulips will rot if allowed to sit in saturated soils for any period of time. They require full sun and do very well in slightly alkaline soils. Tulip bulbs should be removed from the garden after their foliage turns yellow in summer and stored until planting time in your area, which is usually late fall before the ground freezes. This practice is considered too maintenance-intensive by many gardeners who simply buy fresh bulbs each year, treating them like an annual flower.

Hybrid Tulips

Tulipa Darwin hybrids

Zone 4

Type: Spring bulb

Origin: Asia Minor

Habitat: Full sun

Size: 30 inches tall

Plant: Fall, from dormant bulbs

Lord, give me increased patience each and every day. Keep me from hurrying through life at the pace of the world when I should be quietly living at the gentle pace of the heart. Now that I am older, let me take a new look at the world and appreciate the slow and gradual changes that are the essence of the garden. Amen.

He said, "This is how it is with the kingdom of God; it is as if a man were to scatter seed on the land and would sleep and rise night and day and the seed would sprout and grow, he knows not how. Of its own accord the land yields fruit, first the blade, then the ear, then the full grain in the ear. And when the grain is ripe, he wields the sickle at once, for the harvest has come."

MARK 4:26–29

September

Meditation

At one time all plants were wild, and humans through millennia have domesticated many species to grow for food. Corn was once a grassy plant of southern Mexico that the native peoples changed so much over thousands of years that the plant no longer resembles its ancestor. This was among the first genetically modified foods, and in the nineteenth century more ambitious breeding began even though many were horrified at the presumption of man-made hybrids and their potential impact on the preexisting species. The beauty is that God in his wisdom created living things with genes hidden inside them that contain all sorts of characteristics that are recessive and thus not apparent. Who among us can condemn genetic alteration of these plants to harvest the benefits for humankind?

We don't know the extent of the potential of most plants on earth because no one has explored it. It is safe to say that the unknown of astronomical black holes, the murky depths of the ocean trenches, and the microscopic potentials of plant genes can all yield gifts of equal value to humanity.

My father was not a speculative man, and he took Darwin's Origin of the Species *with the same good faith with which he took God's Book of Genesis. God created and Darwin evolved. It was the scientist's job to describe and improve plants and animals of God's garden, while measuring the mountain of knowledge that was there to be scaled. Although he was a Bible Belt fundamentalist, my father believed it was knowledge, not faith, that moved mountains, for in his world there was no mystery that a little midnight oil and mental elbow grease couldn't solve.*

Betty Fussell, *The Story of Corn,* **1994**

Gardening

Every spring we are compelled by some mystical instinct to add new plants to our garden or landscape. In regions with fierce summers and mild winters, fall is the best time to plant permanent trees, shrubs, vines, and even perennials. This timing gives the plants plenty of time to break out of their root ball and become established under winter rains before they are plunged into the rigors of summer. Fall planting is particularly valuable where the climate is hot and dry because it ensures much greater drought resistance in the first year. Where many Southwestern and California native plants are concerned, the fall ushers in their most active growing season. They thrive during the winter rains, peak in spring, and then go dormant for summer. For gardeners in these regions, it may go against your instincts to find new plants and put them in the ground now, but if you do so, you will have greater success with them than if you had planted them in the spring.

PLANT

Indian Corn

Zea mays

Every American is familiar with the white or yellow corn of the produce department, but it is the colorful Indian corn that catches the eye and kindles the imagination. Although we consider Indian corn an ornamental, it was the staple of the New World, the wheat of the Americas, weaving itself into nearly every agrarian culture from Canada to Chile.

This corn is very easy to grow in your garden. Fortunately, you can obtain these Native American strains from heirloom seed catalogs. You can also extract kernels from supermarket Indian corn purchased for the holidays and plant them the following year. Hunt down the dwarf ears that are charming and brightly colored, as they demand less space than the bigger types. The ruby-colored strawberry popcorn also grows well in the backyard and is incredibly bright when first husked. Treat it as you would ordinary corn but do not pick it until fall. Allow the corn plant to turn brown before you harvest so that the ears fully mature and cure on the stalk for better storage. Growing Indian corn is a great project for families who want to bring American history alive in the context of the garden.

Indian Corn

Zea mays

All zones

Type: Summer crop

Origin: North and Central America

Habitat: Full sun, grow in blocks

Size: To 8 feet tall

Notable feature: Edible grain

Plant: Spring, after last frost, from seed

 Lord, you have buried treasures deep within the cells of all living things. Do not allow fear to close my mind to the discoveries which in their own time may benefit the whole human race. Rejecting knowledge is rejecting your creations, and this inevitably leads to suffering. Remind me to think over scientific discoveries and never simply discount them due to my own ignorance. Amen.

Vaquero Priest

Eusebio Kino thought his mission would be with the other Jesuits in China, but he was sent to the New World in 1687 and found his purpose in northern Mexico and the American Southwest. Kino entered the field with a strong background in European agriculture, and as he evangelized the native peoples of the Sonoran Desert, he brought them the skills needed for a more abundant life.

Kino not only knew how to farm but also was a proficient vaquero, known to ride over thirty miles a day at an advanced age in his effort to teach people how to build herds of valuable livestock. He set out to import many new food plants to his villages to augment the three sisters of Native American horticulture: corn, beans, and squash. Kino planted imported apricots, figs, pears, peaches, and pomegranates and instituted the first orchards in the region using old Roman irrigation techniques. More important, he instituted the cultivation of European wheat. His contributions to the Pima and seven other tribes is one of the most enduring legacies of the Spanish colonial era.

"You have heard that it was said, 'You shall love your neighbor and hate your enemy.' But I say to you, love your enemies, and pray for those who persecute you, that you may be children of your heavenly Father, for he makes his sun rise on the bad and the good, and causes rain to fall on the just and the unjust. For if you love those who love you, what recompense will you have? Do not the tax collectors do the same? And if you greet your brothers only, what is unusual about that? Do not the pagans do the same? So be perfect, just as your heavenly Father is perfect."

MATTHEW 5:43–48

September

third week

SEPTEMBER 21 AUTUMNAL EQUINOX

Meditation

Farmers have long governed their activities by the phases of the changing moon and the signs of the zodiac. The sun governed the length of each day with sunrise and sunset. The sun also marks the four seasons at solstice and equinox, defining the span of a solar year. As gardeners, we gradually develop a heightened awareness of these changes and actually sense the season by the length and direction of shadows. Until recently, the sun and its equinox dates governed planting and harvest. So too did the phase of the moon, with planting done during the two quarters when the moon was waxing and with harvesting done only during the quarters of the waning moon. Although science cannot prove if these practices do influence a crop yield, they did help the farmer schedule his tasks.

These old practices show how the tillers of earth were in tune with the heavenly bodies, and they remind us what a magnificent spectacle the sun and moon are in the skies above the garden. At this time when day and night are equal and balance reigns supreme, we are inspired to think of all human beings as being equal to one another. Let the sun by its example show us how to live more humbly because we are all equal in God's eyes.

Gardening

In all but the coldest climates, fall is an ideal time for transplanting because there are many weeks of mild weather to come before winter. Many new gardeners are surprised to discover you can move fairly large shrubs and vines with minimal damage, provided the plants are well cared for after relocation. A few exceptions, such as bougainvillea, are intolerant of transplanting in any season.

Success in transplanting depends on digging out a very large root ball, which is no small task for a sizeable shrub. First, you must cleanly sever roots with a spade around the diameter of the root ball; otherwise you will damage the plant as you tear the roots out of the ground. Starting at that edge, dig a trench around the intact root ball to give you access to the roots underneath. Use a spading fork to work the root ball up from the bottom, cutting the roots cleanly with pruners or long-handled loppers. To prevent disintegration, handle the root ball carefully as you move it. Be sure to set the plant in the new location at the exact depth it was before. Then water generously and keep moist until frost. You can speed healing by applying Superthrive, an inexpensive product that enhances rooting, but do not fertilize the plant until spring.

PLANT

Big Leaf Hydrangea

Hydrangea macrophylla hybrids

The charm of these old-fashioned, summer-flowering shrubs is beyond compare, with more than four hundred different known cultivars. Many species and hybrids are strong autumn bloomers capable of competing with fiery leaf changes. Hydrangeas thrive in partially shaded locations. In milder regions they will thrive in full sun but still demand protection from the wind. The hybrids we grow have a long and complex origin, with a heritage from a host of species, mostly from Asia. They are more easily identified by the type of inflorescence they bear, which is composed of larger, immediately recognizable, sterile male "ray" florets and smaller "perfect" florets bearing both male and female flower parts. A mophead, or hortensia, *H. macrophylla* variety bears only sterile florets in those enormous flowers that are so beautiful freshly cut or dried. The romantic lacecap hydrangea varieties bear a large group of fertile florets in the center of the inflorescence, surrounded by a garland of sterile florets. One of the most remarkable aspects of these shrubs is their reaction to soil acidity, which can turn the flowers blue or make a blue variety more richly colored. To make your hydrangeas turn blue, add aluminum sulfate to the soil.

One who seldom touches the earth, who has no response to its pulsebeats, who shuns the enveloping suns and rains, growth and mysteries is out of tune.

Alfred Carl Hottes, *Facts and Fancies,* **1949**

Big Leaf Hydrangea
Hydrangea macrophylla hybrids
Zone 6 to 7
Type: Deciduous flowering shrub
Origin: Asia
Habitat: Shade or part shade
Size: 3 to 6 feet tall and as wide
Plant: Spring or fall, from containers
Notable Feature: Large flowers suited to drying

Lord, help me to forget the politics of the world that pit one human against the other. Lead me into the garden where equality shines down on me from above. Encourage me to swallow my pride and make amends to those whom I wrong. Remind me often that I am imperfect and that humility is the greatest of all virtues. Amen.

September 22 Feast of St. Phocas, Patron of Gardeners and Gardens

"When you reap the harvest of your land, you shall not be so thorough that you reap the field to its very edge, nor shall you glean the stray ears of your grain. These things you shall leave for the poor and the alien. I, the Lord, am your God."

LEVITICUS 23:22

Phocas of Sinope lived in third-century Greece. He spent his life in the dual acts of prayer and gardening. It proved quite a successful combination, for he grew far more food that he alone could eat. Filled with the charitable spirit of Christ, he shared his bounty with the poor and invited them to come and rest in the peaceful grounds of his garden. He built a small cottage in the garden where weary travelers could rest for the night.

During the brutal persecutions under the Roman emperor Diocletian, the Christian Phocas came under scrutiny, and it was determined he should be executed for his faith. Two soldiers were dispatched to find Phocas, but upon reaching the town late in the day they chose to find lodging in the garden cottage they found outside the city. Its kind owner fed the men, and over their meal they told the gardener the purpose of their visit. Phocas did not reveal his identity but ensured the men had a comfortable bed for the night.

Later that night, he went into his garden and dug a grave in that fertile ground. The next morning he revealed himself to the men, and though they were reluctant to kill such a generous soul, Phocas was duly executed in the garden and buried within it. Recognizing that all organic matter eventually returns to the earth to nourish the soil and other living things, Phocas died knowing that while his soul flew to heaven, his body would feed his garden for many years to come.

Phocas is always depicted as a bearded old man who holds a spade in his hand. An enormous statue of St. Phocas, shown with his tools and wearing the clothes of a farmer, stands in St. Mark's Basilica in Venice.

Meditation

In these times when our fruit trees bear more than we can ever eat, or when we are filled with our squash and tomatoes, it is time to give to charities that cook for the poor. Every parish knows where these kitchens are, and it is there that your overflowing baskets of fresh food can do great work. As Jesus instructed, share your abundance quietly. Deliver it cleaned, boxed up, and ready to eat. It is then that your Father will know the generosity in every gardener's heart.

Finally, I have one message of peace and that is to love one another as God loves each one of you. Jesus came to give the news that God loves us and that He wants us to love one another. And when the time comes to die and go home to God again, we will hear Him say, "Come and possess the Kingdom prepared for you, because I was hungry and you gave me to eat, I was naked and you clothed me, I was sick and you visited me. Whatever you did to the least of my brethren, you did it to me."

Mother Teresa, *A Simple Path*, 1995

Are not five sparrows sold for two small coins? Yet not one of them has escaped the notice of God. Even the hairs of your head have all been counted. Do not be afraid. You are worth more than many sparrows. I tell you, everyone who acknowledges me before others the Son of Man will acknowledge before the angels of God. But whoever denies me before others will be denied before the angels of God.

LUKE 12:6–9

September

SEPTEMBER 29 FEAST OF ST. MICHAEL, ARCHANGEL MICHAELMAS

Meditation

The Feast of St. Michael honors this famous archangel who is depicted as a warrior with his sword. His day is steeped in the folklore of Europe and Britain, where many mountaintop monasteries were erected in his honor. Among the most well known are Mont-Saint-Michel in France, St. Michael's Mount in England, and Mount Gargano in Italy. It is interesting to note that beneath each of these monasteries are ruins of pagan shrines to the sky gods, who controlled the weather. Pre-Christian Europeans no doubt climbed to these high places to honor their pagan gods, and later great pilgrimages were made by Christians. This is likely why Michael's day is connected to the forecasting of rain. Look up into the night skies during the dark of the moon for meteor showers. Then look to the earth for the blossoms that honor St. Michael this time of year: angelica, asters, and autumn crocus.

Climb the mountains and get their good tidings. Nature's peace will flow into you as sunshine flows into trees. The winds will blow their own freshness into you, and the storms their energy, while cares will drop away from you like the leaves of Autumn.

John Muir, *My Summer in the High Sierra*, 1911

Gardening

St. Michael is associated with apple trees because it is during this time when apples are harvested in England and northern Europe. Apples store for the winter better than any other kind of fruit. The traditional way to preserve them is to layer maple leaves for padding in the apple-filled storage boxes. Today we wrap each fruit individually in white tissue or newspaper instead. Now and throughout the harvest season it is important to pick up fallen fruit, whether edible or not. Fermenting fruit is not only smelly; it gives damaging fruit flies a perfect place to reproduce. Wildlife, such as foxes or birds, become tipsy after feeding on fermented fruit. Better to pick up the fruit promptly and add to your compost so that the garden remains clean, up to and beyond the first frost.

PLANT

New England Aster, Michaelmas Daisy

Aster novae-angliae

The flowers of the aster have been likened to stars since earliest times. In Greek mythology the goddess Asteria, looking down upon the earth, saw no stars. She wept, and where her tears fell upon the ground, these plants grew to bloom in a galaxy of starlike daisies. Linnaeus named the genus *Aster* from the Latin for *star,* and it contains a whopping six hundred species that are mostly native to North America and other temperate zones. They are incredible in home gardens because they stand up to the dry heat of late summer and bloom over a long season from late summer to autumn's end. They are always in bloom on the Feast of St. Michael.

The most favored garden species is the New England aster, *Aster novae-angliae,* which can reach six feet and blooms in violet purple. It has many cultivars in various shades of lavender, blue, pink, and red, with the majority growing to less than four feet tall. This variety provides the gardener with a generous palette from which to paint the late-season landscape. Asters are perennials that germinate readily from seed as easily as wildflowers. They may also be divided into new plants every three years to keep them vigorous. Each region of the United States has its own local aster species, and for those who enjoy the beauty and super adaptation of native plants, the asters have plenty to offer.

New England Aster

Aster novae-angliae

Zone 3

Type: Perennial flower

Origin: New England

Habitat: Full sun

Size: Variable, 18 inches to 6 feet tall, to 3 feet wide

Plant: Spring or fall, from containers

The Michaelmas Daisies,
among dead weeds,
Blooms for St. Michael's
valorous deeds.
And seems the last of flowers that stood,
Till the feast of St. Simon and St. Jude.

Anonymous, Traditional English rhyme

Dear Saint Michael, Archangel,
Protect my house and garden from evil as this season of sunlight darkens into winter. Stand guard at the gate, letting no unruly passions, ugly thought, or hint of anger enter there. Please intercede for me to our Lord, Jesus Christ. Amen.

October

Bear's Breech

Acanthus mollis

Zone 7

Type: Half-hardy perennial

Origin: Mediterranean

Habitat: Shade or part shade

Size: To 3 or 4 feet tall and as wide, blooming to 6 feet

Plant: Spring or fall, from containers

Bear's Breech

Acanthus mollis

Many churches and cathedrals of the Old World feature the Corinthian column capital. It is distinguished by a botanical motif, the leaf and flower of the acanthus plant, which is native to Asia Minor and the eastern Mediterranean. The capital's history leads us back to the fifth century B.C. and the Greek sculptor Callimachus, who first designed it. It is said he was inspired by a plant found growing out from underneath a basket left on the grave of a child.

Blessed are the meek,
for they will inherit the land.

MATTHEW 5:5

October

OCTOBER 1 FEAST OF ST. THÉRESÈ OF LISIEUX, PATRON OF FLORISTS

OCTOBER 7 FEAST OF OUR LADY OF THE ROSARY

Meditation

The young nun Sister Théresè of the Child Jesus entered the convent in 1888 at just fifteen years of age and lived there until her death in 1897 at the age of twenty-four. Her brief life was chronicled in her beautiful book, *The Story of a Soul,* published after her death. It tells of her "little way" of simple obedience, which is ever more appealing as our lives grow increasingly complex. Her way was manifest through a special childlike devotion to Jesus, and she viewed her soul and those of all other human beings as flowers of God. She referred to the miracles she would perform after death as "roses from Heaven," and her short cloistered life has indeed left a miraculous worldwide devotion. Her little way is of ever-growing importance, and her roses will continue to fall as she intercedes. Read *The Story of a Soul,* and then if you are so inspired, join the Society of the Little Flower with its devotional circle of roses. You can find out more about the society through its Web site at www.littleflower.org.

Despite the emphasis on and her love of roses, Théresè actually saw herself as a tiny wildflower, which survived the tough seasons of life and blossomed after the cold winter. Wildflowers are often hidden in the forest—few see them, but they give glory to God by just being there and blooming. She knew that not everyone could be a brilliant rose or elegant lily. "If all flowers wanted to be roses, nature would lose her springtime beauty, and the fields would no longer be decked out with the wildflowers."

Robert E. Colaresi, O.Carm, director of the Society of the Little Flower, 1998

Gardening

In October, gardeners in northern states begin preparing for winter. Tender fleshy-rooted plants should be dug up and stored as soon as frost kills back all their green above-ground leaves and stems. If there is still some green, you must wait a bit longer before you dig. Use a spading fork to lift the round corms of gladiolus, tubers of dahlia, and thick roots of canna lily with as little damage to these structures as possible. It's best to start on the outer edge of the plant and work your way under. Inserting the fork close to the center is likely to puncture these structures, inviting rot and disease. The roots and bulbs should be stored in a cool dry place away from frost. Place in trays or boxes on dry coarse sand, moss, or even newspaper, without overcrowding, until planting time comes around again after the last spring frost.

PLANT

Autumn Damask Rose

Rosa damascena

It is believed that *Rosa damascena* was native to Asia and was first brought west by the Egyptians. Remnants of the plants have been found in the Valley of the Kings. It was also grown by the Greeks, who valued the rose as a medicinal and a perfume and spread it along their trade routes. The Romans came upon the rose in the region of Damascus, Syria, hence the species name, *damascena,* and there the mild climate caused it to bloom a second time in autumn. This second bloom was considered miraculous and made the plant highly coveted. The Romans even devised a unique heated greenhouse for the cooler climate in Italy to force this miraculous bloom out of season. This rose has been cultivated since the twelfth century B.C. and is still beloved today. You can order *Rosa damascena* from a heritage-rose catalog or through your garden center. It is considered to be the rose of the Old Testament because of its proliferation in the Holy Land. Since the plant has not changed, you will enjoy the very same flowers that Jesus no doubt admired during his life in Israel.

Autumn Damask Rose

Rosa damascena

Zone 5

Type: Ancient rose species

Origin: Asia Minor

Habitat: Full sun

Size: 6 feet tall and 10 feet wide

Plant: Spring or fall, bare root or from containers

Notable feature: Highly fragrant flowers and leaves

O Little Thérèse of the Child Jesus, please pick for me a rose from the heavenly gardens and send it to me as a message of love.
O Little Flower of Jesus, ask God today to grant me the favors I now place with confidence in your hands. . . .
St. Thérèse, help me to always believe as you did, in God's great love for me so that I might imitate your little way each day. Amen.

October 4 Feast of St. Francis of Assisi, Patron of Animals and Ecology

So the Lord God formed out of the ground various wild animals and various birds of the air, and he brought them to the man to see what he would call them; whatever the man called each of them would be its name.

GENESIS 2:19

Meditation

Saint Francis, the son of a wealthy silk merchant, gave up all worldly things to live in poverty. He founded the Franciscan order, which is based on a meager existence and total devotion to the poor. This dedication was vital because many religious were living in luxury when God called Francis at the crumbling church of San Damiano to repair his church, both literally and figuratively. He and his Franciscans always lived close to the earth, sustaining themselves with what they could grow, gather, or beg as alms. Later in his life Francis would be honored with stigmata, and his humility became legendary. St. Francis was the first to create a Nativity scene in the church at Christmas, only he insisted on live animals. This and many other acts led to his belief that all things of the earth are sacred as creations of God. His statue stands in gardens around the world, for he is seen as the peaceful protector of nature, who likened the brown cloak of the Franciscan to the soft brown plumage of the lark and sparrow.

Francis had a relationship to everything: to man, beasts of the fields and forests, the birds, the fish, trees, flowers, even stones, the sun, the moon, the wind and the stars, fire and water, rain and snow, storms, the earth, summer, winter, and the tender elegy of springtime. With all of these he dealt courteously and admitted them to the circle of his immediate family, for a man who believes in and loves his Creator with his whole heart must also dignify and love all of His creations.

Paul Gallico, "St. Francis and the Animals," from *Saints for Now*, edited by Clare Boothe Luce, 1952

Gardening

Autumn leaves are beginning to fall, but don't mistake them for waste material, because they are a very important source of organic matter. Leaves raked up this month and next should be collected and used to make leaf mold, a valuable soil conditioner and mulch. For a few dollars you can buy an inexpensive product that is used for composting these leaves. It's simply a four-foot-tall strip of heavy black plastic perforated with two-inch diameter holes. Set up takes just a minute. Then start filling the container with leaves, watering and packing them down in layers. Compact them the easy way by letting the kids climb in and jump up and down! You can sprinkle some manure or garden soil between each compacted layer until the whole bin is full. Allow it to sit over winter and by next summer you can strip off the plastic and use the dark, crumbly leaf mold to enrich soil when you plant. Use as many of these bins as necessary to harvest all your leaves and store them out of view in a side or utility yard or at the back of the garden.

PLANT

Crab Apple

Malus hybrids

This remarkable tree rarely goes by species because practically all the plants sold today are hybrids of a dozen or so different species from North America, Europe, and Asia. The Siberian crab apple, *Malus baccata*, which is hardy to -50°F, lends its considerable cold hardiness to many of the showier cultivars, which will survive dips to -20°F. These hybrids are bred to produce a stunning flower show in the spring, followed by brightly colored red, orange, and yellow fruit that stands out in fall and sometimes winter. This fruit is too sour to eat but can be used to make jelly. It is far more valuable as a wildlife habitat. Birds will feed on the abundant fruits, making the off-season garden a place of colorful frenzied activity. The Arnold Arboretum in Massachusetts prefers the variety 'Bob White' for its late-ripening fruit that keeps birds around throughout the coldest months in the North. If St. Francis had grown a plant to feed his dear friends the larks and sparrows, it would undoubtedly have been a crab apple. Francis and his Friars Minor would surely have cut its flowering branches to decorate the church for Easter. Most of all he would have thanked God for creating trees strong enough to take on the winter and continue giving like a Franciscan, all year round.

The lark's garb, her plumage, is the color of the earth. Thus she offers religious an example of how not to wear elegant, flashy clothes, but moderately priced things, of the color of earth, the humblest of the elements.

St. Francis, *Mirror of Perfection*, 113

Flowering Crab Apple

Malus hybrids

Zone 4

Type: Flowering tree

Origin: Many hybrids created in U.S.

Habitat: Full sun

Size: Varies with hybrid—15 to 24 feet tall and as wide

Plant: Spring or fall, bare root or from containers

Notable feature: Fruit feeds winter birds

 All praise be yours, my Lord, through Sister earth, our mother, who feeds us in her sovereignty and produces various fruits with colored flowers and herbs.
  —*St. Francis of Assisi,* Canticle of Brother Sun, *thirteenth century*

And he told them this parable: "There once was a person who had a fig tree planted in his orchard, and when he came in search of fruit on it but found none, he said to the gardener, 'For three years now I have come in search of fruit on this fig tree but have found none. [So] cut it down. Why should it exhaust the soil?' He said to him in reply, 'Sir, leave it for this year also, and I shall cultivate the ground around it and fertilize it; it may bear fruit in the future. If not you can cut it down.'"

LUKE 13:6–9

October

Meditation

Gardeners and farmers label plants and animals that fail to thrive as "poor doers." This sometimes occurs when a plant is slow to get started in life. Roses require at least three years before they start to perform. The tulip tree grows slowly for its first seven years or so, then speeds up considerably. Slow starts can also be caused by conditions such as poor soils or inadequate water, or the plant itself may have been somewhat root bound when first planted. All of these can make a plant a poor doer, but if you rip out a tulip tree after five years of dismal performance, you rob yourself of the more productive years to come.

Many of us are poor doers because our spiritual life has not yet come of age. We may be slow to take root because in our youth there was no desire for a strong faith. We may have once been strong Christians, but conditions have led us to abandon much of our spirituality, stunting our growth. But Jesus tells us that there is time to become stronger in faith and that we should never give up on ourselves. Everyone can evolve beyond merely limping along if we feed on prayer, contemplation, spiritual reading, and the fellowship of others who love our Lord, Jesus Christ.

But my garden is nearer, and my good hoe as it bites the ground revenges my wrongs and I have less lust to bite my enemies. I confess I work at first with a little venom, lay to a little unnecessary strength. But by smoothing the rough hillocks, I smooth my temper; by extracting the long roots of the piper grass, I draw out my own splinters; and in a short time I can hear the Bobalink's song and see the blessed deluge of light and color that rolls around me.

Ralph Waldo Emerson

Gardening

Many new gardeners think that the reason a plant does not survive the winter is that it freezes in the cold ground. Provided that the plant is hardy to your climate zone, frozen earth does not itself damage the plants. The damage actually occurs during spring in the daily freeze and thaw of changing weather. When soil freezes, the moisture trapped within expands, forcing the soil to rise up, or heave. When the weather warms, the ice melts and the soil contracts again, sometimes leaving behind a honeycomb-textured mound of earth. In spring, radical freeze-thaw on a daily basis is brutal on plants. The daily cycle of freeze and thaw is what seriously damages plants by tearing apart the roots. You must think ahead to avoid the problem by mulching now, in the fall of the year *after* the soil freezes. Distribute a thick layer of mulch, such as leaves or straw, over the root zone of the plant. This will insulate the roots and keep the soil at a more even temperature day and night. Around the time of the last frost in spring, remove the mulches to allow the soil to warm up quickly.

PLANT

Maidenhair Tree

Ginkgo biloba

This may be among the most beautiful trees on earth, with its graceful fan-shaped leaves and yellow fall color. It is the only broadleaf among the cone-bearing conifers and is far more primitive than flowering plants. This is so unique a tree in the plant kingdom that it was given its very own family! The ginkgo died out millennia ago in the wilds of China where it originated, and the only trees living today are those grown and perpetuated on temple grounds. Tests on the growth rate of ginkgoes show that they put on but one foot a year for the first ten years and then speed up for the rest of their incredibly long life span. Hardy to zone 5, they are very resistant to pollution and have well-behaved roots, all of which make them a perfect city tree. The ginkgo is also a lovely tree for Asian-inspired gardens or as a shade tree. Since this plant is dioecious, with females producing undesirable fetid fruit, be sure to buy only male trees.

Maidenhair Tree

Ginkgo biloba

Zone 5

Type: Deciduous tree

Origin: China

Habitat: Full sun

Size: 35 to 50 feet tall with equal spread

Plant: Spring or fall, from containers

Notable feature: Unique leaves

 Lord, be patient with me when I fail to grow spiritually. Keep my faith burning strong, not merely lukewarm, and help me never be a poor doer in the eyes of God. While I know that there is time to rekindle my flame, help me to not put it off until tomorrow. Amen.

PIERRE'S GOLDENRAIN TREE

At the mission of the imperial city of Peking, a French Jesuit, Pierre Nicholas le Cheron d'Incarville, found time away from his duties to collect the seed from all the new trees and shrubs he could find in Chinese gardens. In about 1747, d'Incarville encountered a rare caravan visiting Peking and decided to entrust them with his growing collection in hopes it would be delivered as requested to the French botanical garden in Paris, Jardin des Plantes. Among the specimens were the seeds of *Koelreuteria paniculata*, the goldenrain tree, and *Sophora japonica*, the pagoda or scholar's tree, both very popular street and park trees today. All of d'Incarville's seeds germinated in Paris, where they were named and introduced in 1763. Seed was soon distributed to other European botanical gardens, and trees were well established in England and New York City by 1811. This intrepid Jesuit was also credited with the introduction of the tree of heaven, *Ailanthus altissima*, which naturalized in America so well that it became a problem. Planted in many early American cities as a fast-growing shade tree, the aggressive roots destroyed roads and sidewalks. An entire genus of plants, *Incarvillea*, was named for him. It includes a great number of border flowers from Asia with one species, *Incarvillea delavay*, honoring another French missionary priest, Jean Marie Delavay, who worked in nineteenth-century China.

If the firstfruits are holy, so is the whole batch of dough; and if the root is holy, so are the branches.

But if some of the branches were broken off, and you, a wild olive shoot, were grafted in their place and have come to share in the rich root of the olive tree, do not boast against the branches. If you do boast, consider that you do not support the root; the root supports you. Indeed you will say, "Branches were broken off so that I might be grafted in." That is so. They were broken off because of unbelief, but you are there because of faith. So do not become haughty, but stand in awe.

ROMANS 11:16–20

October

Meditation

The olive tree is unique in that though it may be cut down, its root and stump remain very much alive. After a short time, dozens of green shoots will sprout out of the stump and mature into a many-branched tree. Grafting is the ancient art of connecting a twig of one plant with that of another so that they grow together and fuse into a single tree. Olives were grafted in the time of Christ, with the large-fruited varieties grown on the more vigorous root of the wild spiny, small-fruited rootstock. Paul used this as an allegory to explain how the Hebrews represented the wild rootstock, and those who did not follow Christ were sprouts that were broken off, and in their place were grafted rich-fruited gentile twigs. The oil of the olive was among the most valuable commodities in the ancient world, and those civilizations such as the Greeks that could produce it in abundance rose to great power. Paul's choice of the olive tree as a metaphor also suggests that Christianity would produce similar spiritual commodities, which would allow all who believe to be supported by its roots and improve their lives.

There have been many whose lives have been full of thorns, but by believing in the Lord Jesus Christ they have become fruitful. I saw a tree on the mountain once, full of thorns. The man in charge said, "I can change this into a fruitful tree." How could it be done? A few years afterward I went to see it. The gardener had grafted it, and instead of the thorns there was excellent fruit. So the gracious Lord takes us in hand and makes us produce fruit. The Lord came for all, and He can turn sinners into saints, just as in the case of the tree I mentioned.

Sadhu Sundar Singh, *The Cross Is Heaven*, edited by A. J. Appasamy, 1956

Gardening

It is an unpleasant fact that retail plant sellers do not necessarily guarantee cold hardiness in the plants they sell. This is more true of home improvement chain stores than quality garden centers that base their trade on repeat customers and personal service. There is a growing trend to carry semitropical plants, such as bougainvillea, which are treated like an annual flower to grow for just one season. These are expensive, high-color, high-impact plants that make a big splash, but this splash is tempered by a limited life span in cooler regions. You may not realize this when you are drawn to these beauties on display, so do your homework before you buy. You should know your local USDA plant-hardiness zone number and ensure that any plant you buy is appropriate for your zone. If you're not sure, ask the nursery staff whether a particular plant will survive the winter outdoors in your area. If it is not hardy, either prepare to bid it adieu at autumn's end or put it in a pot and find a place for it to winter over indoors. It is possible to dig smaller plants out of the garden and pot them up for winter, but this can be a difficult task with all but the smallest plants.

Japanese Maple
Acer palmatum

In the gardens of Japan, the cherries provide a spring flower display, with the year nicely balanced by an equally vivid autumn maple-foliage color. Over the centuries these small maples have been selected in Japan and later in the West to exhibit a huge range of variation. If a seedling exhibits a new color or leaf shape, it is named as a variety and then propagated by grafting because its seed is unlikely to produce an identical plant. Cuttings are grafted onto a standard maple species rootstock. Japanese maples are fine trees for small city and suburban backyards. They thrive in sheltered locations protected from hot afternoon sun or winds that cause leaf edges to turn brown. These plants enjoy evenly moist soil and look best if gently pruned over time in the Japanese style to enhance their best qualities. Although you can buy the straight *Acer palmatum* species, most of these plants are varieties grouped by their foliage characteristics. The *atropurpureum* group features bronze or purple foliage all year round that grows more intense in the fall. Maples of the *dissectum* group are shorter and feature fancy, lacy leaves that produce a soft, fine-textured effect. Fall is a great time to plant maples because you can choose your plant in full color array to know exactly what to expect in future years.

Japanese Maple

Acer palmatum

Zone 5

Type: Deciduous tree

Origin: Japan

Habitat: Part shade under larger trees

Size: 20 to 25 feet tall with equal spread

Plant: Spring or fall, from containers or burlap

Lord, I pray that in times of need I may draw off your strength and off the strength of all Christians like a weak twig grafted onto a healthy vigorous rootstock. Send your grace to me through the graft union of prayer and communion each day. Amen.

Make no mistake: God is not mocked, for a person will reap only what he sows, because the one who sows for his flesh will reap corruption from the flesh, but the one who sows for the spirit will reap eternal life from the spirit. Let us not grow tired of doing good, for in due time we shall reap our harvest, if we do not give up.

GALATIANS 6:7–9

October

fourth week

Meditation

It is not inaccurate to consider the garden merely a place where we grow plants, but our time there is also spent in contemplation. Every minute you spend among the flowers instead of on the phone, in the car, or watching television is another moment when you sow the seeds of spiritual growth. Farmers are some of the most philosophical people you will ever find, for all those hours spent on tractors must yield a greater understanding of the truths of life. You may think of gardening as a mere hobby, but it is really a spiritual exercise in which we are surrounded by the great natural gifts that lead us to enlightenment. Perhaps it may not seem so at first, but those who have worked the soil for years know that it takes time to yield these inner fruits as well. The monastic traditions of silence and work grew out of this great spiritual path, which feeds the body with physical labor as the mind tills the soft loam of the soul.

*And what a field for contemplation does a garden offer to our view in every part,
raising our souls to God in raptures of love and praise, stimulating us to fervor by the
fruitfulness with which it repays our labor and multiplies the seed it receives;
and exciting us to tears of compunction for our insensibility to God by the barrenness
with which it is changed into a frightful desert, unless subdued by assiduous toil!*

On St. Phocas, patron of gardeners, *Butler's Lives of the Saints,* **CD-ROM**

Gardening

The close of October brings the final spate of chores that ready the garden for winter. What we fail to accomplish now is likely to plague us in the coming spring. A neat and tidy garden means no rubbish piles where damaging insects and pests may find a comfortable home to wait out the winter. It is better that these pests travel next door to find lodging or, better yet, find none at all and vanish altogether with the cold.

Make a point of raking up all the leftover organic matter such as leaves, twigs, stems, fruits, husks, and weeds, and either burn, discard, or compost them. While the offspring of overwintering pests can give birth to a host of young, each weed that is left to go to seed now will infest the spring garden a hundredfold. A single nut sedge plant can produce forty thousand seeds in a season, with other prolific weeds close behind in their reproductive habits. While you really should make the effort to bend and pull the weeds up altogether, if you do no more than merely snap seed heads off the weeds and throw them into the garbage can, you will have taken great strides toward a less laborious effort next year.

PLANT

Creeping Juniper
Juniperus horizontalis

Few plants offer as much as these obliging evergreens and yet are so unacknowledged for their resiliency. This ground-hugging species has produced a variety of cultivars that offer a range of coloring from icy blue to purple-bronze. Hardy to zone 2, an incredible -50°F, these plants will stand up to the most brutal winter. They grow well in extreme heat too and are highly valued in the desert Southwest. Speedy growth ensures that you will be able to cover large bare slopes or neglected strips in glare-absorbing green foliage. These plants are particularly beautiful when planted around boulders or dry streambeds and washes. The branches will spread in an almost feminine way to nestle the stones in a softer, more inviting setting. Conversely, these juniper can be trimmed into tidy geometric forms to create carefree groundcover in a semiformal setting. Once established they are so well adapted we barely see them, but without this carpet the flowering plants would have nothing for contrast save bare ground. For unique color effects, create beds using a number of different cultivars for a patchwork of subtle green hues. Try 'Wiltonii' for silvery blue, 'Emerald Spreader' for bright green, and 'Andorra Compact' for purple-bronze winter foliage contrast.

Creeping Juniper

Juniperus horizontalis

Zone 2

Type: Needled evergreen shrub

Origin: North America

Habitat: Full sun

Size: About 12 inches tall and 6 to 8 feet wide

Plant: Spring or fall, from containers

Lord, as I bid good-bye to the growing season, let me look forward to the restful days of winter. As my activity slows down, remind me to take time indoors for quiet contemplation when I cannot be outdoors among the flowers. Amen.

In pre-Christian Europe, the druids believed that the night of October 31, known as Samhain, marked the transition from fall to winter. For a time the veil between the living and the dead was lifted, allowing the dead to rise and visit loved ones. Celtic peoples celebrated with bonfires to light the way, and the living went about carrying small candles set into hollowed-out cabbages or turnips. In America, these were replaced by more plentiful pumpkins, a distinctly New World plant. When the church deemed November 1 as the Feast of All Souls or All Hallows Day, the night before became known as All Hallows Eve, or Halloween.

November

Northern Maidenhair Fern

Adiantum pedatum

Zone 3

Type: Ground-covering fern

Origin: North America and Asia

Habitat: Shade

Size: 18 inches tall, spreading about 2 feet wide

Plant: Spring or fall, from containers

Northern Maidenhair Fern

Adiantum pedatum

Because this fern grows in the shadow of much larger plants while retaining its elegant beauty, it has become a Christian symbol for humility and sincerity. Native to a large part of the Northern Hemisphere, during the Middle Ages it was dedicated to the Blessed Mother and can be found in shaded Mary gardens today. Maidenhair ferns grow in the grotto fountains of the Vatican and throughout Rome wherever water seeps through the ruins.

You fool! What you sow is not brought to life unless it dies. And what you sow is not the body that is to be but a bare kernel of wheat, perhaps, or of some other kind; but God gives it a body as he chooses, and to each of the seeds its own body. Not all flesh is the same, but there is one kind for human beings, another kind of flesh for animals, another kind of flesh for birds, and another for fish. There are both heavenly bodies and earthly bodies, but the brightness of the heavenly is one kind and that of the earthly another. The brightness of the sun is one kind, the brightness of the moon another, and the brightness of the stars another. For star differs from star in brightness.

So also is the resurrection of the dead. It is sown corruptible; it is raised incorruptible. It is sown dishonorable; it is raised glorious. It is sown weak; it is raised powerful. It is sown a natural body; it is raised a spiritual body. If there is a natural body, there is also a spiritual one.

1 CORINTHIANS 15:36–44

November

NOVEMBER 1 FEAST OF ALL SAINTS
NOVEMBER 2 FEAST OF ALL SOULS

Meditation

In many cultures the Feasts of All Saints and All Souls has become a period when the dead are remembered, whether they lived last week or last millennium. It was instituted on May 15, 615, as the Feast of All Holy Martyrs after the persecutions by the Romans had finally ceased. Although it is assumed that these feasts were set at this time to replace the pagan rite of Samhain, the date actually corresponds to the agricultural seasons. The many pilgrims who journeyed to Rome to celebrate among the graves of the martyrs placed a great demand on a city's food supply. This feast date could better feed them all at harvest than at winter's end. In all the Catholic countries, particularly those in Latin America, these days of the dead can be the most festive yet bittersweet. It is the time to tend the family graves, decorate them with flowers, and wait at night to keep company with their souls. This has become a beautiful celebration that helps the living cope with their lingering grief in the comfort of friends and family. It is always celebrated with flowers, incense made from tree resin, and ritual foods savored by both the living and the dead.

*In Mexico where the "language of flowers" is understood by all, the Orchidaceae
seem to compose nearly the entire alphabet. Not an infant is baptized, not a marriage
is celebrated, not a funeral obsequy performed at which the aid of these flowers
is not called in by the sentimental natives to assist the expression of their feelings.
They are offered by the devotee at the shrine of his favorite saint, by the lover at the
grave of his friend; whether, in short, on fast days or feast days, on occasions of
rejoicing or in moments of distress, these flowers are sought for with an avidity
which would seem to say there was no sympathy like theirs; thus Flor de los Santos,
Flor de Corpus, Flor de los muertos, Flor de Maio, No me olvides (or Forget-me-not),
are but a few names out of many that might be cited to prove the
high consideration in which our favorites are held in the New World.*

J. Bateman, *Orchidaceae of Mexico and Guatemala*, 1890

Gardening

You can employ many tasks to make your garden plants more resistant to winter damage. Conifers that rely on their symmetrical forms or specific shapes, such as upright junipers, false cypress, and arborvitae, can be irreparably deformed by snow loads and winter winds. Cold, dry wind can sear the soft growing tips and cause a brown discoloration. For this reason it is important to protect them with a windbreak set up on the windward side if grown in the open. Snow buildup on these plants can cause side branches to pull away and can permanently disfigure the symmetrical shape. Some tall thin evergreens are wrapped with burlap and tied to preserve their form. Snow falling off the eaves is another source of damage to foundation plants, particularly those with precise forms. They may be protected with a plywood shield, often made in an A-frame form that may be set up free-standing before the first snowfall. Young trees can be badly damaged by hungry rabbits and other rodents that gnaw the tender bark to access the nutritious cambium underneath. Wrapping the trunks with burlap or tree tape not only protects them from the pests, but it also prevents winter sunburn when there are no leaves on the canopy to shade the developing bark.

African or Aztec Marigold

Tagetes erecta

Although they share the same name, marigold, with the calendulas of Europe, Aztec marigolds are a distinctly New World plant. The orange flowering annuals are native to much of Mexico, and when the Spanish brought them to Europe they were first grown in North Africa, hence the name. A smaller species of *Tagetes,* also from Mexico, became the French marigold, as it was first cultivated there. These flowers contain potent oils that are effective insect repellents, and for this reason they are traditionally planted in Latin American fields and gardens to protect the crops. Scientists have proven that the marigolds discourage pests, including soil-born nematodes, tiny worms that infest roots of plants.

The large, orange pom-pom flowers were important in the rites of the Aztecs, and their dead were thought to be able to smell the fragrance. Called *flor de los muertos* in Spanish or *cemachucil* in the Aztec Nahuatl language, they are everywhere in Latin America during the three days of *Todos Santos,* or Day of the Dead. These plants deserve much greater attention from gardeners for their meaningful religious associations, beauty, and value in natural pest control.

Aztec Marigold

Tagetes erecta

All zones

Type: Summer annual flower

Origin: Central America

Habitat: Full sun

Size: To 30 inches tall and 24 inches wide

Plant: Spring, from seed or containers

Notable feature: Repels insects in kitchen garden

Lord, bring your saints into my garden to remind me each day through their examples. Let St. Francis inspire me to love the birds and all living things. Let St. Phocas the gardener be my guide in enriching the soil. Through St. Thérèse, the Little Flower, may I make every act, no matter how small, one that honors you. Amen.

Then he told them a parable. "There was a rich man whose land produced a bountiful harvest. He asked himself, 'What shall I do, for I do not have space to store my harvest?' And he said, 'This is what I shall do: I shall tear down my barns and build larger ones. There I shall store all my grain and other goods and I shall say to myself, "Now as for you, you have so many good things stored up for many years, rest, eat, drink, be merry!"' But God said to him, 'You fool, this night your life will be demanded of you; and the things you have prepared, to whom will they belong?' Thus will it be for the one who stores up treasure for himself but is not rich in what matters to God."

LUKE 12:16–21

November

Meditation

Everywhere you look there is an explosion of gardening products. Tools, decorative objects, and all sorts of new materials fill the garden center. You can spend a fortune on all of this, with novice gardeners often falling prey to gimmicks and hype. You must remember that the essence of the garden is plants and that they are both the most crucial and the most affordable component. Until recently, a gardener would buy little beyond the basics, and an ability to grow from seed or propagate one plant into ten new ones fleshed out a landscape for pennies. We've diverged from this self-sufficient form of gardening and become too focused on products at the expense of plants. As it is in the garden, so it is in life, for it is not the fine car but the journey; it is not expensive clothes but the people we gather with while wearing them; and it is not the size of the IRA but the freedom it grants.

Who owns the blue vault overhead? Who owns the south wind? Who owns the sun's rays that make our planet a comfortable place in which to live? Who owns the rain that refreshes our plants and makes them grow? Who owns the energy that changes cold soil to living plants, and thence to animals? Who owns the birds and flowers? Who owns the brush that transforms the leaves from their summer green to garnet, carmine, copper and gold? Is this not wealth that is not capable of being made private property, certainly not transferable, and all the better that it cannot be so?

Letter from Charles B. Wing, in Alfred Carl Hottes, *Garden Facts and Fancies*, 1949

Gardening

You may be surprised to find that many plants, from roses to chrysanthemums, will root very easily on their own wherever branches come in contact with the soil. This is a natural way for the plant to reproduce itself, and it offers us the simplest and least risky way of multiplying a favorite plant.

This technique is called layering and is most often applied to plants that produce long vinelike stems or runners. A plant may take up to a year to produce roots from an ordinary cutting, but by layering you can shorten this to just weeks in a ready-to-root plant such as a chrysanthemum. Rather than stake a flexible stalk, allow it to flop down to the soil. Choose the most likely point of contact with earth and gently scratch the underside to create an abrasion that is quicker to root as it heals. Add rooting hormone to the wound to further speed the process. Then pin the limb to the soil with a U-shaped piece of clothes hanger. Cover the limb with sand or loose, peaty garden soil and then forget about it for a few months. Go back to check the progress by uncovering the limb, and if roots have developed, simply sever the limb from the mother plant and either pot it up or transplant it to its new location.

PLANT

Chrysanthemum

Chrysanthemum x *grandiflorum* hybrids

Chrysanthemums are an autumn-flowering perennial cultivated in China before the seventh century B.C.; by the tenth century A.D. there were at least twenty known cultivars. Since then, more than two thousand colors and fancy flowered forms have been developed in Asia, and most of these are well adapted to our American gardens. Mums prefer full sun and even watering to bloom through the fall until frost. If you grow the tall exhibition mums with the large single flowers, you will have to stake the lanky plants, or they will flop over. Many people don't want to bother and prefer to plant the compact florists mums, which produce an abundance of flowers that make better seasonal garden color. The cold hardiness of this immense clan can vary, so be sure to find out from the garden center whether you should treat the new plant as an annual or a perennial. It is a common practice to divide mums in the spring after new shoots come up by cutting off clumps from around the edges of the parent plant. You can layer mums anytime during the summer, but be sure to leave yourself enough time to get the new plants into the ground and give them time to settle before the first frost.

Chrysanthemum

Chrysanthemum x *grandiflorum* hybrids

Zone 5

Type: Autumn-flowering perennial

Origin: Japan

Habitat: Full sun

Size: 1 to 3 feet tall and 2 to 3 feet wide

Plant: Spring or fall, from containers

Help us, O Lord, to grasp the meaning of happy growing things, the mystery of opening bud and floating seed—that we may weave it into the tissue of our faith in life eternal.
        —Alfred Carl Hottes, Garden Facts and Fancies, *1949*

Jesus went around to all the towns and villages, teaching in their synagogues, proclaiming the gospel of the kingdom, and curing every disease and illness. At the sight of the crowds, his heart was moved with pity for them because they were troubled and abandoned, like sheep without a shepherd. Then he said to his disciples, "The harvest is abundant but the laborers are few; so ask the master of the harvest to send out laborers for his harvest."

MATTHEW 9:35–38

November

Meditation

The life of a religious is much like that of a dedicated gardener. While the former views all things through the lens of faith, the latter sees everything through connections to the plant kingdom. It is amazing to discover how pervasive plants are in our world, for they define our sense of place, feed us, and provide shelter and medicine. Beyond being merely useful, they improve our daily life by offering us the chance to arrange beauty and color and to act as the cocreators with God of our compositions. No matter how long one remains steeped in horticulture, there are always new plants to discover and new qualities or nuances of familiar ones to realize. There is no end to what one can learn about plants, making them a lifelong interest that never ceases to enrich us. And perhaps it is here that the religious and the gardener meet again, for our understanding of human spirituality is also ever expanding, and inner growth continues every day until death. Literally and figuratively we serve the same master, with one reaching him through the living body of Christ and the other finding Christ through the green living bodies of his creations.

If thy heart were right, then every creature would be a mirror of life and a book of holy doctrine. There is no creature so small and abject but it reflects the goodness of God.

Thomas à Kempis, ***The Imitation of Christ***

Gardening

As we slide into winter and the garden has been safely put to bed, our thoughts soon turn to the coming spring. The best way to start off this season of rest is to order some of the best gardening catalogs now, ahead of time, so that you have them when you find time to sit in front of the fire and peruse their pages. Even if we buy little or nothing from a catalog, they can fill us with inspiration and the desire to grow. It's important to understand the range of catalogs so that you order those that best suit your needs. Specialty catalogs sell just one kind of plant, such as bulbs or potatoes or fruit trees. Heirloom catalogs are the most fun because they are a romp through the history of horticulture, making available old-fashioned varieties with astounding vigor. Kitchen-garden catalogs present an incredible range of greens, vegetables, and herbs for seasoning that you will rarely find at a retail garden center. Nonplant catalogs sell ornaments, clothes, specialized tools, products, and organic supplies. Before you order the same tired general catalogs, investigate the specialties and order as many as you can so that you are well provisioned for the postholiday doldrums.

PLANT

Red Twig Dogwood

Cornus stolonifera

Drive through the suburbs of Chicago during the barren winter and you'll find little color evident. Yet here and there, in foundation plantings and in hedges, a haze of bright red twigs leaps out of the landscape. They are the red twig dogwood, a shrubby form of that tree that is native to North America from Washington State to Maine and from Canada to Colorado. Its extreme cold tolerance to zone 2 means there is no place too cold for them in the United States, but they may suffer in warm winter regions for lack of chill. Red twig has much more to offer in spring, when shrubs bloom with clusters of small white flowers followed by decorative fruits in summer. These fruits are of superior wildlife value, drawing birds and small mammals into the garden. During late fall the red twig dogwood exhibits a superior red-orange foliage change. Because this shrub is native, it will grow on natural rainfall within its range and needs no special care, but without an occasional pruning it can reach the size of a small tree. Best of all, you can cut the red twigs and bring them indoors for bright winter-holiday decorations.

Red Twig Dogwood

Cornus stolonifera 'Sibirica'

Zone 2

Type: Deciduous shrub

Origin: Asia

Habitat: Full sun or part shade

Size: 9 feet tall and 5 feet wide

Plant: Spring or fall, bare root or from containers

 Without grace, I am nothing but a dry tree, a barren stock fit only for destruction. Therefore, O Lord, let Your grace always lead and follow me, and keep me ever intent on good works, through Your Son Jesus Christ, Amen.

— *Thomas à Kempis,* The Imitation of Christ

Thanksgiving

"He brought us out of Egypt with his strong hand and outstretched arm, with terrifying power, with signs and wonders; and bringing us into this country, he gave us this land flowing with milk and honey. Therefore, I have now brought you the first fruits of the products of the soil which you, O Lord, have given me." And having set them before the Lord, your God, you shall bow down in his presence. Then you and your family, together with the Levite and the aliens who live among you, shall make merry over all these good things which the Lord, your God, has given you.

DEUTERONOMY 26:8–11

Meditation

There is no doubt that a strong parallel exists between the Old Testament Israelites and the Pilgrims who first settled New England. One fled enslavement in Egypt and then faced a long journey in the desert, and the other fled religious persecution and had to survive a brutal first winter in the New World. Little is reported on the exact conditions of the Pilgrims who arrived late in the year at Plymouth, Massachusetts, their people starving onboard the *Mayflower* after the Atlantic crossing. When they first anchored offshore on November 11, 1620, a party went ashore and found an Indian graveyard where, like manna, baskets of corn had been left as gifts for the dead. They would spend the winter in crude shelters, cold, sick, and starving. Half of these settlers did not see spring. These realities add more meaning to that first harvest feast in the New World. Despite the hardships, the faith of the Pilgrims never lagged. Just as God instructed the Israelites to celebrate their "land flowing with milk and honey" by feasting with the "aliens who lived among [them]," the Pilgrims also celebrated their great feast with Native Americans who had shared their agricultural knowledge. It is likely that the Pilgrim leaders read the passage in Deuteronomy 26 before that historic meal.

Our corn did prove well, and, God be praised, we had a good increase
of Indian corn, and our barley indifferent good, but our peas not worth the gathering,
for we feared they were too late sown. They came up very well, and blossomed,
but the sun parched them in the blossom.

From unnamed Pilgrim's diary

> "For six years you may sow your land and gather in its produce. But the seventh year you shall let the land lie untilled and unharvested, that the poor among you may eat of it and the beasts of the field may eat what the poor leave. So also shall you do in regard to your vineyard and your olive grove."
>
> EXODUS 23:10–11

November

Meditation

God's edict in Exodus that the field shall lie fallow the seventh year is not merely a charitable act but an approach supported by soil sciences of the twentieth century. Even more interesting is that the man who would develop the concept of crop rotation knew his Bible well and quoted from it. George Washington Carver of the Tuskegee Institute declared, "The primary idea in all my work was to help the farmer and fill the poor man's empty dinner pail." Carver was thinking about poor farmers of the South struggling to eke out a living on exhausted cotton fields. Perhaps this Old Testament passage ignited the fire that would revolutionize agriculture. Had Carver not been such a devout Christian, his program of fortifying the land with legumes, namely peanuts, and rotating crops to feed the soil would never have yielded such benefits to humanity.

*I indulge in very little lip service, but ask the Great Creator silently daily,
and often many times per day to permit me to speak to him through the three great
Kingdoms of the world, which He has created, viz. the animal, mineral and
vegetable Kingdoms; their relations to each other, to us, our relations to them
and the Great God who made all of us. I ask Him daily and often momently
to give me wisdom, understanding and bodily strength to do His will,
hence I am asking and receiving all the time.*

**George Washington Carver, *George Washington Carver in His Own Words*,
edited by Gary Kremer, 1987**

Gardening

The key to successful organic gardening and farming is to use a variety of practices that fortify the soil naturally. The technique known as green manuring is rooted in Carver's contributions to agriculture. Plants known as legumes have a unique ability to take nitrogen out of the air and fix it into the soil through their roots, which explains why the lawn is always greener around the clovers. When a legume plant is tilled back into the soil it adds another boost of stored nitrogen, just as animal manures do, and the plant parts themselves add valuable organic matter to the soil. Green manuring involves tilling the remains of the summer crop into the soil during the fall, then sowing a cover crop of legumes such as clovers, beans, or peas, all of which belong to the pea family and prefer the cooler "off" season. In late spring the mature cover crop is tilled directly into the soil before the growing-season crop is sown. Gardeners or farmers need do nothing more than sowing and tilling to boost soil productivity in a natural, organic way. For anyone who grows a kitchen garden or wishes to improve the soil quality on a larger piece of ground, sow a cover crop of green manures. Seed can be obtained from most garden centers or from the catalogs listed at the back of this book.

Lupine

Lupinus Russell hybrids

The beautiful spires of blooming lupine are often the most eye-catching perennials in the garden. As members of the legume clan, they have the ability to fix nitrogen in soil. The genus name is related to their Old World title as "wolf" flowers because they were thought to chase away other plants. This is not true, however; lupines simply colonized soils so lacking in nitrogen that no other nonlegume was able to grow there.

Do not lie in a ditch and say, God help me; use the lawful tools He hath lent thee.

George Chapman, *May-Day,* **1611**

These showy hybrids were developed from perennial wild-flowers that thrive in cool summers. This makes them hardy to zone 3, ideal for the north and for mountainous regions. Lupines produce huge spires of flowers up to three feet tall, in every color of the rainbow. Russell hybrids do not perform well in hot, dry climates, but the native purple-flowered North American perennial lupine, *Lupinus albifrons,* makes a fine substitute.

Hybrid Lupine

Lupinus Russell hybrids

Zone 3

Type: Perennial flower

Origin: North America

Habitat: Sun in northern states, part shade in southern states

Size: 18 to 20 inches tall and as wide

Plant: Spring or fall, from containers

As the rain hides the stars, as the autumn mist hides the hills, as the clouds veil the blue of the sky, so the dark happenings of my lot hid the shining of thy face from me. Yet if I may hold your hand in the darkness, it is enough. Since I know that, though I may stumble in my going, you do not fall.

—From the Gaelic, translated by Alistair MacLean,
Oxford Book of Prayer, *1985*

PLANT

Autumn Osmanthus

The Chinese do not see a man in the moon as we do but the image of an osmanthus shrub or *gui* flower. An ancient folktale explains that Wu Gang, an immortal, was banished to the moon for infidelity and there he eternally tries to chop down the osmanthus, which has the power to continuously heal its wounds and is undamaged by the ax. Occasionally, on bright nights, the lunar osmanthus sheds its rare, shiny seeds, which shower down to earth in the form of shooting stars, so prevalent in the meteor showers of autumn.

The best known species in the West is *Osmanthus fragrans,* which was first identified and named by missionary priest Jan Loureiro, 1715–96. His accurate classification, which is the earliest botanical classification recorded in that formerly closed empire, is a reference that stands to this day. A more cold hardy *Osmanthus* that is just as fragrant is *Osmanthus delavayi,* discovered in Yunan province a century later by the famous Jesuit missionary botanist Jean Delavay. Of the stock of seed he sent to French nurseryman Maurice de Vilmorin around 1890, only one seed germinated in the garden of the Paris School of Arboriculture. From this individual, all new plants were propagated. This variety remained rare well into the twentieth century until new seed was brought from China.

Sweet Osmanthus

Osmanthus fragrans

Zone 8

Type: Evergreen shrub

Origin: China

Habitat: Full sun, part shade in southern states

Size: 10 feet tall and 6 to 8 feet wide

Plant: Spring or fall, from containers

Notable feature: Highly fragrant flowers

December

English Hawthorn
Crataegus laevigata, 'Paul's Scarlet'
Zone 5
Type: Deciduous flowering tree
Origin: Europe
Habitat: Full sun
Size: 15 to 20 feet tall and as wide
Plant: Spring or fall, from containers
Notable feature: Spring flowers,
winter fruits

Hawthorn

Crataegus coggygria

Legends state that Joseph of Arimathea, in whose tomb Christ was

buried, left Jerusalem in the first century and sailed to Britain.

Making landfall, he was so ill he crawled up from the beach and

planted his staff in the soil. The staff grew into a hawthorn tree

that bloomed at Christmas, rather than in spring. Sprigs in full

bloom were carried throughout the realm in winter so that all the people

could see and be converted. While seemingly miraculous, Joseph's hawthorn

is a Holy Land species with a different season of bloom.

He shall judge between the nations,
> and impose terms on many peoples.
They shall beat their swords into plowshares
> and their spears into pruning hooks;
One nation shall not raise the sword against another,
> nor shall they train for war again.

O house of Jacob, come,
> let us walk in the light of the Lord!

ISAIAH 2:4–5

December

ADVENT

Meditation

Plowshares and pruning hooks, implements of agriculture, became the hallmark of peace in the ancient world. The plowshares represent cultivated earth, and pruning hooks the tools that render wild plants into domestic production. What better way to welcome the Prince of Peace than to transform the instruments of death into those that bring life and sustenance to humanity. More important, these tools symbolize the transition the Israelites made from a pastoral nomadic people to a people settled and cultivating their promised land.

Gardening

A great number of tender perennials are treated like annual flowers in the north. Annuals are planted in spring and grow until frost, when they die. But in milder winter climates, plants such as geraniums and impatiens will live outdoors for years, and even if slightly frost burned will recover and flourish in spring. This is the time to bring the last of your potted plants indoors before they are killed by a hard frost. Choose a south-facing window where they will receive the maximum amount of light during the winter months. Arrange a bench or table at the level of the sill where the pots may sit with optimal exposure. They are unlikely to grow much or flower, but they will happily sit dormant, waiting for the days to lengthen in spring. Bringing plants indoors is a great way to extend the seasonal garden and save money by preserving your geraniums, impatiens, and other long-lived summer flowers.

PLANT

English Holly

Ilex aquifolium

English holly is the consummate holiday decorating plant. Despite its common name, the species is actually native to Europe and Asia Minor, not just to England. The ancients regarded this plant as specially blessed, for it is among the few plants that remain evergreen in the northern regions. With the advent of Christianity, the red berries became a symbol of the blood of Christ and the prickly leaves his crucifixion wounds. This holly is dioecious, which means a male pollinator is needed if the more-decorative female forms are to produce berries. Among the females are a number of different cream or gold variegations that make superior decorating material even when fruit is absent. Scatter a number of different types into the landscape for convenient holiday decoration. These plants are slow growing and often trimmed to shrub size, but the species can reach as high as 60 feet tall with age. Cultivars can be much smaller. While these plants stand up nicely to coastal winds and cool weather, they do not tolerate hot or dry conditions.

English Holly

Ilex aquifolium

Zone 6

Type: Evergreen shrub, small tree

Origin: Europe

Habitat: Full sun

Size: 15 to 25 feet tall and 10 to 12 feet wide

Plant: Spring or fall, from containers

Notable feature: Christmas decorations

O thou who covers your high places with the waters,
Who sets the sand as a bound to the sea
And does uphold all things:
The sun sings your praises,
The moon gives you glory,
Every creature offers a hymn to you,
His author and creator, for ever.
    —*Eastern Orthodox,* Oxford Book of Prayer, *1989*

But a shoot shall sprout from the stump of Jesse,
and from his roots a bud shall blossom.
The spirit of the Lord shall rest upon him:
a spirit of wisdom and of understanding,
A spirit of counsel and of strength,
a spirit of knowledge and of fear of the Lord.

ISAIAH 11:1–2

December

Meditation

This Old Testament prophecy of the birth of Christ, the Messiah, is followed in verse six by a declaration of change: "The wolf shall be a guest of the lamb, and the leopard shall lie down with the kid; the calf and the young lion shall browse together, with a little child to guide them." These changes in the natural order of predator and prey illustrate that God as creator of all living things assigns this order of the universe. Only he has the power to alter that order, and though changes are symbolic in these verses, they remind us that there is an ingenious order or interconnectedness to all living things. Whether of plant or animal, insect or microscopic organism, this divine order is so profound that all who understand its extensiveness can never again deny that a higher power is at work. Even the pagan Roman philosopher Seneca declared, "What else is nature but God, and divine reason residing in the whole world and its parts?"

*Blessed be you, harsh matter, barren soil, stubborn rock; you who yield only
to violence, you who force us to work if we would eat. Blessed be you, perilous matter,
violent sea, untamable passion; you who unless we fetter you will devour us.
Blessed be you, mighty matter, irresistible march of evolution, reality ever new-born;
you who, by constantly shattering our mental categories, force us to go ever further
and further in our pursuit of the truth. Blessed be you, universal matter, unmeasurable
time, boundless ether, triple abyss of stars and atoms and generation:
you who by overflowing and dissolving our narrow standards of measurement
reveal to us the dimensions of God.*

Teilhard de Chardin, S.J., 1881–1955

Gardening

There is but one plant in our gardens that stands out as a true parasite: mistletoe. It grows on the limbs of deciduous hardwood trees, drawing off the moisture and nutrients of its host. When the trees are bare for the winter you can see the mistletoe clearly, and now is the best time to cut it out. A single clump of it can infect an entire tree if you try to cut and remove the mistletoe when it still bears its gluey fruit; remove it only when fruit is absent. You may either hire a tree-care professional to cut it out, or if it is accessible and you are nimble, cut it out yourself. One method is to cut off the limb that bears the mistletoe at least two feet above the mistletoe stem to ensure it does not come back. If that will disfigure the tree, cut off the stem itself and then apply a special mistletoe-killing product to the stump to keep the plant from growing back. It is interesting to note that mistletoe most often infects trees that are weak, and when the parasites spread to many places in the canopy they together draw off enough energy to kill their host. Mistletoe is poisonous and is best kept out of the reach of pets and children.

North American Mistletoe
Phoradendron serotinum

This parasite is similar to its cousin in Europe, from which much of our holiday mistletoe folklore originates. Ancient tribal peoples, who believed it was imbued with great powers, called it "a different twig." Extensive rites involved cutting mistletoe at the winter solstice and hanging it in the house as a talisman. This plant was entrusted to the care of Venus, goddess of love, which explains why we kiss under the mistletoe. Because of the pagan source of these holiday traditions, mistletoe is not often seen in Christian churches.

Lord, I am like to mistletoe,
Which has not root and cannot grow
Or prosper, but by that same tree
It clings about; so I by thee.
What need I then to fear at all
So long as I about thee crawl?
But if that tree should fall and die,
Tumble shall heaven so down will I.

—*Robert Herrick, 1591–1674*

December 12 Feast of Our Lady of Guadalupe

A great sign appeared in the sky, a woman clothed with the sun, with the moon under her feet, and on her head a crown of twelve stars. She was with child and wailed aloud in pain as she labored to give birth.

REVELATION 12:1–2

Meditation

She stands upon a crescent moon, the stars are scattered on her turquoise veil, and she wears the *cinta* of a pregnant woman. So does the image of Our Lady of Guadalupe resemble the "woman clothed with the sun" who would galvanize the faith of Latin America. Her story is one of roses and of cactus on the rocky Tepeyac Hill, a few miles from Mexico City. She instructed the humble Juan Diego to gather the roses in his agave-fiber cloak, or *tilma,* and carry them to the bishop. Not only was it a miracle that roses even grew on Tepeyac and did so in December, but they left on that cloak an image of a dark-skinned Indian Virgin Mary. She told Juan and the Mexican people, "Do not be troubled or weighted down with grief. Do not fear any illness or vexation, anxiety or pain. Am I not here who am your Mother?" Though woven of agave fiber that lasts but forty years at the most, this *tilma* on display for all to see in the new basilica in Mexico City is clear, colorful, and miraculously intact four centuries later.

> *Resting amid parti-colored flowers*
> *I rejoiced; the many shining flowers*
> *came forth, blossomed, burst forth*
> *in honor of our mother, Holy Mary.*
>
> **Juan de Zumarraga,**
> **Bishop of Mexico, 1531**

She sent me to the hilltop where I have always seen Her, to pluck the flowers that I should see there. And when I had plucked them I took them to the foot of the mountain where She had remained, and She gathered them into her immaculate hands and then again into my mantle for me to bring them to you. Although I knew very well that the hilltop was not a place for flowers, since it is a place of thorns, cactuses, caves and mezquites, I was not confused and did not doubt her. When I reached the summit I saw there was a garden there of flowers.

The words of Juan Diego quoted by Luis Lazo de la Vega, 1649

In 1531, Bishop Zumarraga of Mexico prayed to Mary that the Aztecs would be peacefully converted, and he asked her to send him Castilian roses as a sign that his prayer was heard. It is believed that the roses on Tepeyac Hill were not the small native wild rose but *Rosa damascena* of Castile, Spain, which Zumarraga immediately recognized when Juan Diego opened his cloak to reveal the miraculous image.

You brought a vine out of Egypt;
>   you drove away the nations and planted it.
You cleared the ground;
>   it took root and filled the land.
The mountains were covered by its shadow,
>   the cedars of God by its branches.
It sent out boughs as far as the sea,
>   shoots as far as the river.

PSALM 80:9–12

December

DECEMBER 21 WINTER SOLSTICE

Meditation

Imagine what it must have been like before electricity during this darkest time of the year. Imagine living in a house with small windows and having only the light of a candle or an oil lamp on a cloudy winter's day. It would be a challenge just to read a book, and your body would respond to this denial of sunshine with a sort of mild seasonal depression. Imagine if you were an illiterate European peasant filled with superstitious dread that the sun may never return! No wonder both pagans and Christians created festive celebrations at this time to drive away the winter darkness with living evergreen plants and the color red—the color of heat and empowerment. These plants became the symbol of promise that the sun inevitably returns, and there is no more naturally beautiful way to herald the birth of the Redeemer. Though rooted in paganism, the use of natural plants is fitting, for it reminds us of our ties to the earth and all living things, which are creations of God.

Christmas in church and home, even in our prosaic and mechanical age, is almost inconceivable without the presence of the delightful evergreens. If their use at such a time did not possess the sanction of high antiquity, it would be sufficiently recommended by its own inherent beauty. But this is one of the happy contributions which paganism made to the Christian festival. The graceful custom has its roots in the profound reverence of the ancients for all natural phenomena.

William Muir Auld, *Christmas Traditions*, 1931

Gardening

During the winter, you'll need to engage in a number of tasks on a regular basis. First, snow can cause serious damage to evergreen plants when it is allowed to pile up on top of them. A small evergreen may be broken under the weight and never regain its original form. When it is snowing heavily, go out occasionally and brush off any accumulated snow around foundations and in the landscape to protect your shrubs and small trees from damage.

Second, ashes from a woodstove or fireplace are valuable to the soil. They are rich in potash, and bits of charcoal make a good amendment for opening up heavy soils. If the ground is bare you can sprinkle them around the garden each time you clean out the fireplace or woodstove. You can also store them in watertight containers to distribute onto the soil just before you till it for the spring garden.

Finally, coming up with last-minute holiday decorations is made easier if rosemary grows in your garden. Select perfect red apples and cut two-inch-long sprigs of stiff rosemary. Stud the apple with sprigs of rosemary about one inch apart and then use a clothes hanger to pierce the center of the apple. Form an eye with needle-nose pliers and tie a ribbon to it. Hang apples over the fireplace where rising heat will release the savory aroma of rosemary and apple.

PLANT

White Fir

Abies concolor

This beautiful symmetrical evergreen tree is very cold hardy to zone 4 and grows well in Harvard University's Arnold Arboretum, where it is considered a superior tree. The species is native to mountain ranges of the western

United States. It grows slowly and will reach 120 feet at maturity. Its beauty is in its stiff, pyramidal form, which makes it a fine evergreen for landscaping. Blue-silver foliage stands out dramatically against a background of deep green pines, hemlocks, or cedars. The boughs are particularly beautiful as holiday decorations. For smallish gardens the variety *Abies concolor conica* retains a shorter stature that is more versatile. When planted in a front yard, this variety is an excellent candidate for outdoor Christmas lighting. These trees are free of any known pests or diseases and withstand both heat and drought far better than other hardy conifers.

White Fir

Abies concolor

Zone 4

Type: Needled evergreen tree

Origin: Western United States

Habitat: Full sun

Size: To 120 feet tall and 40 feet wide

Plant: Spring or fall, from containers

Lord, as my life becomes holiday-hectic, remind me that your birthday is to be celebrated not in stores or while battling traffic or by racing around at the last minute. When I forget that your coming is more important than material things, let the scent of evergreens, the vivid red of poinsettia, and the fragrance of the feast continually remind me that your coming is at hand. Amen.

The Christmas tree as we know it originated in sixteenth-century Protestant Germany from the older tradition of the fruit-laden paradise tree. Martin Luther promoted the use of the fir tree. The Christmas tree spread to Britain and then America with German immigrants in the eighteenth century. While it was accepted in homes, it did not appear inside churches until much later.

In the beginning was the Word,

> and the Word was with God,

> and the Word was God.

He was in the beginning with God.

All things came to be through him,

> and without him nothing came to be.

What came to be through him was life,

> and this life was the light of the human race;

the light shines in the darkness,

> and the darkness has not overcome it.

JOHN 1:1–5

December

DECEMBER 25 CHRISTMAS *DIES NATALIS DOMINI*

Meditation

A great deal of folklore surrounds Christmas night and how all of creation paused at the moment of Jesus' birth. It is said that the cattle fell to their knees, as did the deer in the forest. Bees awoke from their winter sleep to hum a hymn of praise to the Christ child. The birds sang all night, and the lowly sparrow sang in the lilting voice of the nightingale. And all the trees and plants on the banks of the River Jordan bowed in reverence toward Bethlehem. The Holy Night is one in which we treasure tradition, honor generosity, and remember the most important event in the history of humanity. No wonder all of nature pauses, for we cannot conceive of life without our Lord.

Gardening

In Europe, people were especially kind to their domestic animals at Christmastime, for the creatures had been present in the stable at this momentous event. St. Francis encouraged this practice both on the farm and for the wild things in nature struggling for food in the barren winter. This time of year, the birds in your area will need all the food they can get to stay alive in the cold. Ordinary birdseed may seem helpful, but it takes more energy to digest, with relatively low nutritional value. The avid bird lover will offer higher-quality pickings that maximize nutrition. Hulled raw sunflower seeds, ground peanuts, and bread crumbs are all excellent for winter birds. Suet, which you can buy in blocks, is valuable for many species. Bird-conscious gardeners grow sunflowers and put the dried seed heads out into feeding stations at intervals throughout the winter. Remember that if you begin feeding winter birds at Christmas, don't stop after the holidays, but keep it up until spring. By then the birds will share your home and will remain there to feed on undesirable insect pests and keep your landscape healthy.

Poinsettia

PLANT

Euphorbia pulcherrima

This, the most beautiful plant of Christmas, is a native of Mexico and ranges across the equator to South America in the lower elevations where the winters rarely taste frost. Forced in North American hothouses to produce color over the holidays, in Latin and South American gardens they can reach fifteen feet in height. The plant is a member of the *Euphorbia* genus, which all have a poisonous milky latex sap. Its coloring is not derived from the flower but from specialized leaves known as bracts that surround a cluster of very small, insignificant blooms. Day length and temperature cause the green leaves to take on their red coloring, which was coveted by the Aztec princes and used to produce vivid dye. The princes could not grow the plants in the cooler climate of high-altitude Mexico City but had them brought at great expense to the palaces there for decoration. Red flowers, the color of blood, held great significance among this pre-Columbian people. The plant was

brought to North America by Joel Poinsett, American minister to Mexico, and has retained his name ever since. The holiday poinsettia is often thrown away after the holidays, but if kept out of cold or drafts, it can be watered and fed for many months of enjoyment.

Poinsettia

Euphorbia pulcherrima

Zone: Tropical

Type: Flowering shrub

Origin: Mexico

Habitat: Full sun

Size: 10 feet tall, spreading as wide

Plant: Anytime, from containers

Notable feature: Hothouse Christmas plant

What shall we offer you, O Christ, who for our sakes has appeared on earth as man?
Every creature made by you offers you thanks. The angels offer you a hymn; the magi, gifts; the shepherds, their wonder; the earth, its cave; the wilderness, the manger:
And we offer you a Virgin Mother. O God from everlasting, have mercy on us.

　　　　　　　　　—*Eastern Orthodox prayer*, Oxford Book of Prayer

Resources

Plant and Garden Supply Catalogs

The Antique Rose Emporium
9300 Leukemeyer Road
Brenham, TX 77833-6453
(800) 441-0002
www.antiqueroseemporium.com
Excellent resource for old roses and "found" heritage roses well suited to southern gardens.

Irish Eyes—Garden City Seeds
P.O. Box 307
Thorp, WA 98946
(509) 964-7000
www.irish-eyes.com
The *best* source of seed potatoes and heirloom varieties.

Native Seeds/SEARCH
526 N. Fourth Avenue
Tucson, AZ 85705
(520) 622-5561
www.nativeseeds.org
A nonprofit organization that appreciates $1 for a catalog. Extraordinary source of heirloom seed from Native American peoples of the Southwest and Northern Mexico.

Old House Gardens
536 West Third Street
Ann Arbor, MI 48103-4957
(734) 995-1486
www.oldhousegardens.com
Fun, well-written, user-friendly supplier of heirloom bulbs of all kinds.

Peaceful Valley Farm Supply
P.O. Box 2209
Grass Valley, CA 95945
(888) 784-1722
www.groworganic.com
Tools and supplies for organic farmers and gardeners.

Roses of Yesterday and Today
803 Browns Valley Road
Watsonville, CA 95076
(831) 728-7901
www.rosesofyesterday.com
Excellent selection of old rose varieties.

Seeds of Change
P.O. Box 15700
Santa Fe, NM 87506-5700
(888) 762-7333
www.seedsofchange.com
Excellent source of organic heirloom varieties with excellent on-line catalog as well as annual printed catalog.

Select Seeds Antique Flowers
180 Stickney Hill Road
Union, CT 06076-4617
(860) 684-9310
www.selectseeds.com
Colorful, information-packed catalog of old-fashioned flowers and heirloom plant seeds.

Territorial Seed Company
P.O. Box 157
Cottage Grove, OR 97424-0061
(541) 942-9547
www.territorial-seed.com
Full range of contemporary and heirloom kitchen-garden plants well adapted to cooler northwestern climates. Includes good choices of colorful kales and peas.

Recommended Books on Christian Gardens

Earth Prayers, edited by Elizabeth Roberts and Elias Amidon
HarperSanFrancisco, 1991

Mary's Gardens, by Vincenzina Krymow
St. Anthony Messenger Press, 1989

Plants of the Bible, by Harold N. and Alma L. Moldenke
Dover Publishing, 1986 republication of 1909 edition

Rooted in the Spirit, by Maureen Gilmer
Taylor Publishing, 1997

Glossary

annual A plant that germinates from seed, matures, flowers, and sets new seed before it dies within the span of a single year or growing season.

bare root Trees, shrubs, or vines that have been grown in the field. While dormant they are dug up and shipped for sale with roots exposed. These are sold for planting only during the dormant season, which is early spring in the North and midwinter in the South.

biennial A plant that lives for two years or two growing seasons. Grows from seed in the first season and may flower modestly. By the second season the plant reaches its mature size, flowers, and sets seed. Well-known biennials include foxglove and hollyhock.

biopesticide By studying the bad bugs, scientists discover good bugs large and small that naturally kill unwanted pests without chemicals. The most well known is BT, a microscopic nontoxic virus that kills caterpillars. Another example is packaged live ladybugs, which when released in the garden will feed on aphids, thus controlling their populations naturally.

bolt Leafy plants such as cabbage and lettuce grow into dense, leafy clumps of foliage. When they go to seed, or bolt, often with the heat of summer, the stem inside elongates to create a tall spike that flowers before the plant dies.

bulb A fleshy, underground storage structure for certain plants such as tulip or hyacinth. During the growing season, energy is stored in the bulb to fuel the growth and flowering of the plant the following spring.

catkin While bee-pollinated plants produce flowers, many wind-pollinated plants produce catkins. These unusual structures, often seen on maple and oak trees in the early spring, hang in pendulous clusters from the bare branches where wind can easily catch and transport the pollen.

chinoiserie A style of design inspired by the buildings and gardens of China. It extends to furniture and other decorative arts of eighteenth-century Europe.

compost All organic matter from leaves to melon skins are subject to decomposition, leaving behind a by-product called humus, or compost. It is used to enrich soil for plants.

conifer A group of mostly evergreen plants bearing needlelike leaves with seeds in woody cones. Common examples are pines and firs.

container-grown Nursery plants that are grown and sold in pots.

corm A small, dense bulblike structure from which plants grow.

cultivar A specific named variety of a plant, usually the result of breeding.

cultivate To till the soil, grow plants.

damping-off A fungal disease that attacks young seedlings at ground level, causing them to rot. Typically occurs in infected soils coupled with overcrowding and dampness.

deciduous Plants that shed their foliage at the end of the growing season before going dormant for winter. They regrow all their leaves again in spring.

determinate Often used to describe varieties of tomatoes that produce their fruit all at once. This ensures a large quantity convenient for commercial or home canning. *See* indeterminate.

dieback The death of branch tips by any means. Often caused by dehydration of cells immediately adjacent to a cut limb or rose cane.

dioecious Plant in which male and female flowers are born on different plants. Requires one plant of each sex in the vicinity to result in fruit or fertile seed on the female.

evergreen Plant that retains its foliage all year around.

first frost A general term for the first killing frost of fall, which causes most herbaceous plants to die back.

flat file A carpenter's file, also known as a bastard file, used to sharpen tools.

foundation planting Plants arranged around the outer walls of a house to provide attractive framing and to screen off ugly footings, vents, utility meters, and crawl spaces.

graft union The point at which a plant is grafted. The union is composed of rootstock below and scion wood above. The scion wood is the named variety.

grafting The art of uniting the wood of a new plant onto twigs or branches of an old one.

green manuring The practice of improving soil over a large area by using plants known as legumes. These share the unique ability to increase soil nitrogen while alive, and their remains boost nitrogen a second time when tilled in.

ground cover Plants used in masses to cover bare ground with foliage and flowers.

habitat garden A garden or part of a garden filled with plants and flowers attractive to desirable wildlife such as butterflies, bees, hummingbirds, and songbirds.

hard frost Temperatures low enough to cause soil to freeze.

heaving soil The result of hard frost at night followed by daytime thaw, which causes soil to expand and contract. Expansion is not damaging to plants, but the repeated freeze and thaw of spring is very hard on tender roots.

heirloom Old-fashioned plant varieties that have been replaced by more modern ones. These rediscovered antiques are horticultural treasures preserved only by continuous cultivation.

hybrid The offspring created by crossing two different species within the same genus.

indeterminate Indeterminate tomatoes flower and set fruit over a much longer season for continuous fresh supply in smaller quantities. *See* determinate.

kitchen garden Gardens large or small devoted to edible vegetables, roots, fruits, and culinary herbs.

layering A no-risk method of plant propagation often used with vines by pegging the runners to the ground. At this contact point they produce roots, then the new plant with roots is separated from the parent.

limbing Cutting off the lower branches of a tree to reveal the trunk.

marginal A group of plants, usually reedlike, that are adapted to conditions along the edges of waterways. They survive fluctuating water levels that alternate between inundation and drought.

mulch Organic matter or other material spread out on the surface of the soil. Mulch reduces weed growth, helps retain soil moisture, and insulates plant roots from heat. Mulch is also applied to plants after the ground freezes in fall to protect from spring freeze-thaw damage.

nut sedge A pernicious weed that should never be allowed to survive in any garden. It is nearly impossible to remove once established.

organic gardening Creating and tending gardens free of any synthetic chemicals, fertilizers, or pesticides.

ornamental plant Plant grown strictly for its beauty and contribution to environmental quality.

perennial An herbaceous plant that lives for many years.

phosphorus The nutrient in fertilizers that contributes to flower and fruit production.

pot-bound A plant that has grown in a pot for too long and as a result has a dense, impacted root system.

pruning Specific cutting and shaping of plants, often to alter form or to promote greater fruit production.

rhizome A horizontal stem or root that travels underground to extend the area of a plant by sprouting at points along its length.

rock garden Gardens with rapid drainage and full exposure, created with rocks or masonry that are suited to plants of alpine origin.

root ball The mass of roots and soil connected to a plant.

rooting hormone Product used to artificially speed up the generation of new roots from a plant cutting.

root zone The area underground that encompasses the entire root system of a plant.

runner A general term used to describe the long, flexible branches of a vine.

seedling A relative term for a very young plant newly sprouted from a seed.

shade garden A composition of plants that prefer to grow in the shadows of trees and structures.

sucker Rank, whiplike growth that sprouts at the base of a tree or shrub trunk. So named for its ability to suck growth energy away from more desirable parts of the plant.

taproot A single, very strong root that grows straight down into the soil. The taproot is valuable anchorage for trees and accesses moisture deep in the soil for drought resistance.

trellis An open structure that provides an ideal climbing surface for vines. Ranges from tight lattice to open, lightweight fan or grids affixed to a wall.

water garden A composition of aquatic plants that live submerged or partially submerged in a pool or pond.

wetland Water-related ecosystems, such as swamps, marshes, fens, seeps, and bogs.

windbreak A row of evergreen trees or shrubs planted close together in order to reduce windy conditions on the lee side. Often used on the coast or plains to protect homesites, orchards, and roadways.

zone A standardized map system created by the United States Department of Agriculture to designate the maximum cold winter temperatures across the United States. It encompasses ten different zones with the coldest, zone 1, experiencing temperatures below -50°F and the warmest, zone 10, which never dips below 30°F. These zones allow the plant industry to designate the universal climatic limitation of any plant.

Zone	Minimum Temperature
1	Below -50°F
2	-50°F to -40°F
3	-40°F to -30°F
4	-30°F to -20°F
5	-20°F to -10°F
6	-10°F to 0°F
7	0°F to 10°F
8	10°F to 20°F
9	20°F to 30°F
10	30°F to 40°F
11	40°F to 50°F

About the Author

Maureen Gilmer is a gardening expert, landscape designer, writer, nationally syndicated columnist, photographer, television personality, and horticultural consultant. She has appeared on ABC's *The View,* CBS's *The Early Show,* Discovery Channel's *Home Matters,* and HGTV's *Way to Grow* and *Willard Scott's Home and Garden Almanac.* She has published more than fifteen books on gardening, landscaping, and the environment, including *The Gardener's Way, Rooted in the Spirit,* and *Gaining Ground.* Her articles and photographs have appeared in such periodicals as *Country Living, Better Homes and Gardens, Horticulture, Fine Gardening,* and *Garden Design,* and her weekly color column, "Yard Smart," is syndicated nationwide by Scripps Howard News Service. She is the landscape features columnist for the *Sacramento Bee* and the garden expert for CBS news affiliate KOVR-13, Sacramento. She created and maintains MoPlants.com, which averages fifteen thousand hits per month. She lives in southern California with her husband, Jim.

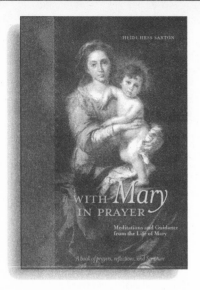
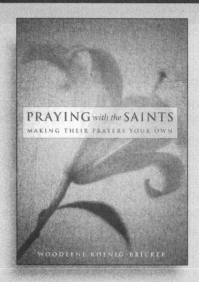